Picture the Past

NOTTINGHAM

Picture the Past
NOTTINGHAM

Geoffrey Oldfield

breedon **books**
PUBLISHING

First published in Great Britain in 2007 by
The Breedon Books Publishing Company Limited
Breedon House, 3 The Parker Centre,
Derby, DE21 4SZ.

ISBN 978-1-85983-577-7

Printed and bound by Cromwell Press Ltd, Trowbridge, Wiltshire.

CONTENTS

INTRODUCTION

In the past, anyone wanting to view the collections of hundreds of thousands of old images in the libraries and museums of Derbyshire or Nottinghamshire would have to travel many miles to try and track down the ones they were interested in. This proved to be frustrating and time consuming for researchers, a barrier to anyone from further afield as well as damaging to the more fragile images from all the handling. The collections include photographs, slides, negatives, glass plates, postcards and engravings recalling the history of our local communities for a hundred years and more.

Thankfully senior staff in four local authorities got their heads together to solve the problem and the idea of conserving the images using digitisation while at the same time giving people all over the world access to the digitised versions was conceived.

Funding was obtained from the Heritage Lottery Fund at the beginning of 2002 together with additional cash from the four partner authorities, Derbyshire and Nottinghamshire County Councils and the City Councils of Derby and Nottingham. Local studies staff in the libraries and museums started collating images and information ready for inclusion in the project and sent out thousands of letters requesting copyright clearance from the original photographers or their relatives. Nick Tomlinson was appointed as project manager to lead a team of experienced professionals inputting the information into a custom-built database and carefully digitising the images.

The Picture the Past website (www.picturethepast.org.uk) was launched in June 2003 and by the end of 2006 in excess of 63,000 pictures had been added. It now attracts well over 10,000 visitors from all over the world viewing thousands of pages of images every month. The site is updated on a regular basis and actually gives the user the ability to 'correct' existing information or add more information to those pictures with scant details.

The website is designed to be as 'easy to use' as possible and includes a simple keyword search facility as well as more comprehensive search mechanisms for users looking for images with a particular theme or by a specific photographer. Visitors can print out low resolution copies for their own personal use or study purposes but for those users wanting to own a top-quality glossy photographic copy the website includes an online ordering service. Thanks to the involvement of *Derby Evening Telegraph*, this enables users to browse the collection and order and pay for their selections securely online. The prints are produced on state-of-the-art equipment and, as a non-profit making project, all the income raised from this service goes back into the conservation and preservation of more original pictures.

This book gives you the chance to sample just a handful of the images contained in the website and it is very much hoped that you will go on to enjoy the rest of the pictures on the website.

For people who do not have access to the Internet at home, or who are not sure where to start, there are computers available for public use in all libraries and the local studies staff are more than willing to help you get started.

The website can be viewed at **www.picturethepast.org.uk**

Picture Website Wins National Accolade

'Picture the Past' continues to go from strength to strength with success in a national awards programme for local history publishing. The website won the Alan Ball Local History Award in 2004 in recognition of its commitment to local history publishing.

The awards are made every year by the Library Services Trust to public libraries and local authorities who – through books, magazines, websites or any other form of the written word – promote their communities' local history.

Michael Saich, Chairman of the Library Services Trust, presented the award on 19th January 2005. He remarked 'Picture the Past was successful in competition with both print and non-print entries in gaining one of the main awards. The Trust was impressed by how successfully the partners worked together to create the website and we feel it is important for local authorities to continue to produce publications of such a high standard.'

INTRODUCTION

In 1841 Alfred Barber, a professional photographer, opened the first photographic portrait studio in Nottingham, at Bromley House, Angel Row. Due to financial, legal and technical difficulties, no further studios were opened until 1854. In a directory dated 1864 under the heading 'Artists', 13 of the names were marked as 'photographic'.

The use of photographs for personal use soon became popular, particularly for the richer and fashionable classes. At the same time there is evidence to show that amateurs and others were taking outdoor photographs of scenes such as the Market Place. The use of photographs as a form of artistic expression soon spread, with the formation of societies. The use for commercial purposes and for illustrating books also grew and towards the end of the 19th century the advent of coloured picture postcards for sending messages meant a considerable increase in photography of outdoor scenes and events. Photographs were recognised as historic records early in the 20th century, and Nottingham Public Libraries started to collect those that were offered to them and later took steps to obtain photographs depicting the great physical changes in Nottingham – new buildings, demolition of old ones and changes in transport.

In 1976 the County Council, which had become the library authority for both city and county, opened a new Central Library in a former shop on Angel Row. The premises included a separate local studies section, building up a large collection of illustrations including photographs, books on local history by Nottinghamshire authors and information on all kinds of local interest. These included a large collection of index cards, microfilms and microfiches and more recently computers with access to the internet.

The illustrations collection has become recognised as an indispensable aid to illustrate books of local interest and also by members of the public with an interest in records of the past. To further this interest, the Nottinghamshire Library has become a member of the North East Midland Photographic Record along with other public libraries in the region. They have mounted a major operation to make their illustration collections available on the internet, under the title 'Picture the Past'.

The publishers of this book have obtained the permission of the Photographic Record to extract, via the internet, some 400 photographs relating to the City of Nottingham, of which there are a total of nearly 9,000 images. Each one has been described in a caption.

Nottingham City Council

Bromley House, Angel Row. The first Nottingham photographic studio was in this building. An extension was built on the south flank for it.

BASFORD

The Anglo-Saxons found the short stretch of the River Leen to their liking and formed several settlements on its banks. Basford was one of these and like the other villages this proved to be of use for modern industry, which started in the 18th century. Basford was able to use the River Leen for the manufacture of hosiery on stocking frames and of lace in the 19th century. Bleaching of the yarn and finished goods became one of Basford's specialities. It also helped the village to grow with increased population and number of houses, especially as it was near to Nottingham which was growing rapidly.

At the first national census of 1801, Basford's population was 2,124 and by 1831 it had increased to 6,325. This was the figure for the whole parish, which was a large one and some of the growth in population occurred in new settlements away from the River Leen – New Basford, Carrington and Sherwood. By 1871 the total population of the four villages was 13,038 and in 1877 they were added, along with Lenton, Radford and Sneinton, to the borough of Nottingham.

They had all become more urban with the increased population requiring schools, churches, chapels and factories. Other important factors were the coming of the railways, collieries and building of more modern roads. This chapter deals with the original part, now known as Old Basford, later chapters illustrating the growth of the other parts of the parish.

Photography became more widely used from the 1890s onwards and most of the photographs of Old Basford date from then onwards. The 20th century saw a considerable change in Old Basford's industry, especially in the older textile trades and in the closing of the coal mines. A major change in the appearance of the old parts was the large-scale demolition of the out-worn 19th century houses and the building of new ones.

Nottingham Historical Film Unit

Basford House Gates

The ornate gates were erected when Basford House on Church Street was built in the early 1700s. It is of brick and is a listed building. It was the home in the mid-18th century of Alderman Thomas Langford, five times Mayor of Nottingham and a wealthy goldsmith. In the 19th century Thomas Bailey lived here. He was an author, historian and one time newspaper owner. Later, it became the home of the Spencer family, two of whom were clerks for the *Basford Guardian*.

A.P. Knighton

Basford Cemetery

This picture is from a coloured picture postcard and would have been taken about 1900. The cemetery had been opened by Basford Local Board on six acres of land on Nottingham Road at the junction of what later became Perry Road. In 1877 when Basford was incorporated into the borough it became part of its burial grounds. It soon became full and some years ago the two chapels were damaged by fire.

L. Cripwell

Basford Vicarage

Up to 1881, Basford Vicarage was listed in directories as being on Radford Road, between the Gas Works and the Sanitary Wharf. In September 1881 the Borough Council approved the building of a new vicarage, based on a plan submitted by James Fowler, the Diocesan Surveyor. The site was at the west end of Old Basford Cemetery (above).

There were no other buildings on the site, but in the 1920s Perry Road was extended from Hucknall Road to Nottingham Road.

A.P. Knighton

Lincoln Street Level Crossing

In 1848 the Midland Railway opened a branch line along the Leen Valley with a station at Basford. The level crossing was for traffic coming from Arnold. When Vernon Road was built it would have become busier. Now the tram from Nottingham to Hucknall helps to delay traffic as well.

The tall building in the centre of the picture was the Butcher's Arms public house. All the buildings on the right were demolished in the 1970s.

A.P. Knighton

Vernon Park

In 1900 Nottingham City Council agreed to buy an 18¼ acres estate, including a large house, Vernon House, from Mr Charles James Cox for £18,780. There was an ornamental lake, fed by the River Leen, woodland and open land. Vernon Park was erected with sports facilities and the lake was retained and is still there.

From the style of dress of the girls in the picture it would appear to have been taken soon after the opening.

Nottingham Historical Film Unit

Vernon Road

This photograph was taken after 1912 as the shops are listed for the first time in a directory of that date. The view is looking north and the newsagent's shop was at the corner of Acton Avenue. After Basford, Bulwell and Radford became part of the borough in 1877, a new through road from Alfreton Road to Bulwell was constructed. Basford's section was called Vernon Road and Bulwell's Highbury Road.

George L. Roberts

Alice Square

This photograph was taken in 1964 when the clearance scheme was being carried out. The entrance to Alice Square was between 13 and 15 Queen Street.

Nottingham City Council

44th Nottingham Scout Troop Headquarters

This picture is described as being taken in 1926, the building being at the corner of Cowley Street. It was originally a Primitive Methodist Chapel but later was a wicker furniture factory.

The troop was founded about 1916, mainly due to the efforts of George Stocken. Later, a local builder named Noah Hopewell converted the building for the troop. The building was demolished as part of the Old Basford Clearance Area and the troop was provided with a new headquarters in 1976 on Lincoln Street.

Nottingham City Council

Western Boulevard Bridge

This photograph has been precisely dated 8 April 1923. An outer ring road was built from Middleton Boulevard along Western Boulevard, where the bridge was built to cross the railway line. An existing road bridge seen just beyond the new bridge connected Vernon Road with Church Street.

The ring road was completed by building Valley Road from Nottingham Road to Mansfield Road, with Fairfax Street linking Western Boulevard with Nottingham Road.

Ellis School

Opened in 1931 on a former allotment site on Bar Lane, Ellis School was one of a new type of school known as central schools. Adjoining Ellis, which was for boys, was a similar building for girls, Guilford. Ellis was named after John William Ellis, a Nottingham MP and industrialist who did much to influence education in the late 19th century, while Guilford commemorated Sarah and Hannah Guilford who undertook much voluntary work to improve social conditions.

Wicklow Street

This photograph was taken just over 50 years ago, in 1954, for the City Council as part of the action to be taken for the next 20 years to demolish the 30,000 or so 19th-century houses. They were mainly no longer fit to live in because of their poor condition and lack of modern facilities. The picture graphically reveals how the outside of the rear of such houses were used.

BULWELL

Like Basford, which it adjoined, Bulwell was one of the settlements on the banks of the River Leen. It remained a small agricultural village until the 18th century when the textile industry, based at first on the stocking frame, started to grow.

At the census of 1801 it had a population of 1,585 compared with Basford's 2,124. The latter grew to 6,352 by 1831 while Bulwell only grew to 2,611. *White's Directory* of 1832 gives an informative description of Bulwell in that year. It records it as 'a populous village where there are three bleach works, a lace thread mill, three corn mills, several extensive quarries and kilns and a number of stocking frames and bobbin net machines'.

Bulwell is four miles from the centre of Nottingham and did not have a common boundary with the borough, which probably meant that Bulwell grew more slowly than other adjoining areas. Moreover, both Bulwell and Basford were finding that the River Leen, for so long a source of great use, was becoming a nuisance. Pollution, both from domestic and industrial use, increased to become a health hazard. However, the Borough in 1877 obtained an Extension Act to bring Bulwell and five other areas within the area. This meant a common effort to govern the enlarged borough ensured that Bulwell, like the other areas, could be improved.

It also meant that there was more land available for new housing as the population continued to increase throughout the whole borough. Another benefit which helped Bulwell was the construction of a continuous new road from Trent Bridge to Bulwell, linking the borough with Radford and Basford as well. Highbury Road was the part in Bulwell. Although there had been a railway line with a station at Bulwell, this had probably been of more use for freight than for passengers. The new road meant that road traffic increased and for passengers horse-drawn buses and trams were developed and in 1901 electric trams.

These changes meant greater facilities for employment, shopping and growing leisure outlets – music halls, theatres and sport. Between 1871 and 1901 the population of Bulwell increased from 4,276 to 14,767. This resulted in the erection of 2,000 or so new houses and more in the period from 1900 to 1914.

After a cessation in building during World War One, a new departure in the provision of new houses was the start of building council houses. Bulwell had two of the earliest estates at Bulwell Hall and Highbury Vale. Most of the new houses were built on open land, but a start was made on demolishing some of the older houses which were becoming unfit and had out-of-date facilities such as outside toilets.

These trends continued after 1946 and another factor affecting Bulwell was the changing pattern of industry. Coal mining and quarrying ceased and the textile industries of lace and hosiery affected Bulwell as well as other parts of the city. More large-scale clearance of unfit houses took place from the 1960s in one part of Bulwell, between Oxford Street and Latimer Street. The cleared sites were developed with modern houses, flats and bungalows in a way that obviated through traffic. At the same time land to the west of the market place saw the creation of new houses at Crabtree Farm and Snape Wood.

The creation of a new bypass road enabled the market place and part of Main Street to be pedestrianised. A bus station was built and more recently the Nottingham to Hucknall tram has changed travelling habits. Although there has been some new light industry, which has been created on the outskirts, Bulwell has become, like other suburbs, mainly residential with retail, service and leisure facilities.

Strelley House

Also known as the Old Grammar School, this picturesque building was erected under a trust deed dated 1667. It was provided by George Strelley, who lived at Hempshill, to provide education for up to 30 children. It did so until 1867, since when it was used for various purposes. It is now a private house and is probably the oldest building in Nottingham used as a private residence.

F.W. Stevenson

Brockclose Yard

This photograph was dated 27 May 1913 and is of Nos 3 to 11 Brockclose Yard, which was on the north side of Main Street near Duke Street. The yard and the houses have long since gone.

Bulwell Hall

The hall was built in 1770 by John Newton and was at first derisively called Pye Wipe Hall. It stood in extensive grounds near the border of Hucknall. In the 19th century it became the home of the Reverend Alfred Padley, although he was not the vicar. In 1908 it was purchased by the Corporation and the grounds laid out as a public park, with a golf course and other sports facilities. The hall was used for a time as a home for tubercular children with an open-air school. It was later used as an approved school and demolished in 1958.

Nottingham City Council

Nottingham City Council

River Leen Bridge

This photograph is dated 1885 and shows Station Road, which connects Main Street with Highbury Road. The Robin Hood railway line and the Nottingham to Hucknall tram track are crossed by a new footbridge. St Mary and All Souls Church tower can be seen in the background and in the centre is the Horse Shoe public house, which is still there. Most of the other buildings have been demolished.

Nottingham City Council

Red Lion Public House, Coventry Road

There was a Red Lion public house listed in an 1832 directory, the landlord being Dowager Brummit. The horse bus in the picture was used to connect Bulwell to Basford in 1901 when the photograph was taken. The purpose was to link up with the trams until they came to Bulwell a little later.

Nottingham Historical Film Unit

Bulwell House, Main Street
Bulwell House was No. 70 Main Street and appears to have been a large house in a fashionable style. The photograph was taken from the bottom of Ravensworth Road, a gated private road leading to Bulwell Hall. It was occupied in 1891 by Robert Buckby, aged 34, a physician and surgeon.

The house was demolished before 1907 when a building plan was approved for the erection on the site of a Salvation Army Hall.

Nottingham City Council

Aslin Yard, Main Street
Although this photograph is stated to be Aslin Yard, this is not a street name but it is described as being a wheelwright and blacksmith's yard, Star Inn. From directories and the 1901 census No. 45 Main Street was occupied by Thomas Aslin, wheelwright. No. 47 was the Star Inn. It seems, therefore, that the almost rural scene was behind the Inn. In 1901 Nos 1 to 53 Main Street were between Coventry Road and Vere Street, but most were demolished some years ago.

Helmet Yard, Hazel Street

There were only six houses in Helmet Yard, which was on the east side of Hazel Street. The photograph was taken by public health inspectors of the City Council in 1913. The chalk marks on the door would have been made by the inspectors prior to demolition. In the 1901 census 23 people lived in the six houses, one of which was occupied by a coal miner, his wife and seven children. A son, aged 13, worked as a pottery wedger and a daughter, aged 16, as a lace dresser.

Nottingham City Council

Nottingham Historical Film Unit

St Mary's School, Main Street

The photograph is thought to date from the early 20th century. Before the Education Act of 1871, many of Nottingham's schools were founded by the Church of England, hence the name of the school. The first part had been erected in 1866 and extended in 1872. The building is still used as a primary school with its original name, although the tower and spire shown in the picture have been removed.

Methodist Church, Main Street

There were Methodist churches in Bulwell early in the 19th century. The building in the photograph was of a Methodist New Connexion circuit. The foundation stones give the date of laying as 7 August 1882, two of which were laid by Aldermen of the Borough, Edward Goldschmidt and Edward Gripper.

In the 1980s the building became a Greek Orthodox but is now a Seventh Day Adventist Church.

Highbury Vale

This was one of the council house estates built by the Nottingham City Council under the Housing Act 1919. The photograph shows some of the houses on Highbury Road, on the east side. The first contract, for 38 houses, was completed in April 1922. More houses were built later extending the estate to Brooklyn Road. The photograph was taken about 1925 and tram lines can be seen. The road in the centre of the picture is Laxton Avenue.

Nottingham City Council

Henry Mellish School

This school on Highbury Road, although in the city, was built by Nottinghamshire County Council as a secondary (later grammar) school for boys aged from 11 who lived outside the city. It was named after the chairman of the County Education Committee. After 1944 it became a comprehensive school. In 1998 when the council once more became the education authority, it formed part of the education system.

F.W. Stevenson

Coventry Road

This photograph was taken in 1930 and shows the different types of houses. The last of them were demolished a few years ago when the High Road was built to divert traffic from the Market Place and Main Street.

CARRINGTON AND SHERWOOD

Both Carrington and Sherwood were created early in the 19th century. Unlike Basford, Bulwell and other areas surrounding Nottingham, they were not villages that had been settled in Anglo-Saxon times. Both were created by landowners building new houses on land that had not been built on before. This was because they were part of Basford parish, which covered 2,894 acres of land and had a population of 2,124 in 1801. The original settlement on the River Leen was almost on the edge in the west, but the parish stretched for almost two miles eastwards to Mapperley.

Most of the land had not been cultivated and was like heath or moor land. In 1792 an Enclosure Act was obtained which re-allocated the land to the existing landowners in lots. These could then be improved for cultivation or sold or leased for building on. There was the Nottingham to Mansfield turnpike road through the eastern part of the parish, the south end of which was only a mile from Nottingham market place. The period from 1801 to 1821 had seen a large increase in the population of both Nottingham and Basford due to the introduction of the lace trade in these areas, especially when a patent for a bobbinet machine expired. This was recognised by some of the landowners, who started to sell some of their land. On 28 February 1825 an auction of 20,000 square yards of land took place, the site being adjacent to the west of the turnpike road with the junction of what was the road to Bulwell, now Hucknall Road. There was a plan showing the 40 lots available and how new streets were to be laid. Houses were soon built, mainly for men who could work on the new machines, and the area was given the name Carrington. This was because one of the landholders was a member of the Smith banking family, who had been granted a peerage with the title Lord Carrington.

About the same time land was similarly sold just under a mile further up the turnpike road, on what today is Elmswood Gardens. To distinguish it from Carrington this part was called Sherwood, due to its proximity to Sherwood Forest.

Both these new suburbs started to grow, Carrington more quickly than Sherwood. By 1832 there were 32 bobbinet makers and 20 other trades such as joiners, blacksmiths and shoemakers. There were also two academics and four public houses. Later a market place was built and in 1841 St John's Church followed. Although most of the increased population in both parts were mainly working classes, the nearness of Nottingham soon encouraged owners of factories and businessmen whose establishments were in Nottingham to come to live in what directories at one time described as 'handsome villas'. Carrington's growth officially ended at Haydn Road, but the two places increasingly became more or less as one large suburb. In 1877 both became part of the borough, as did the rest of Basford parish and the other adjoining villages.

Sherwood continued to expand westwards from Mansfield Road, as it became known when the turnpike ceased. The extent of the development by 1877 is clearly shown by a map drawn up for the borough engineer Marriot Ogle Tarbolton. Connection with the town became easier when horse-buses were provided which were later to be overtaken after 1901 by electric trams, the first line and depot being at Sherwood. A suburban railway line started in 1889 along a circuitous route through Sneinton and Mapperley but was not successful. This is perhaps not surprising, as the Sherwood station was at the top of the steep Winchester Street.

The Great Central Railway was much more successful with two stations, one on Haydn Road and the other near Gregory Boulevard. The 1920s saw the first City Council housing estate built at Sherwood, an outer ring road, Valley Road and Woodthorpe Park. The textile industry gradually diminished, but there were some newer industrial buildings particularly on Haydn Road. Sherwood contributed to Nottingham's needs with a prison, a workhouse and later its two major hospitals.

Little remains of the original settlements but with a prepondance of private housing, Sherwood and Carrington today are a popular residential suburb with shopping and other facilities.

Spring Terrace, Carrington

Selkirk Street, on the west side of Mansfield Road, was one of the first streets to be built in the new village of Carrington. Spring Terrace had 18 houses on the south side of Selkirk Street. It would have a common yard between the odd and even houses when built but this photograph is dated 1914 after improvements had been carried out, including fencing between houses.

Nottingham City Council

St John's Church, Carrington

As Carrington was in Basford parish its church, St Leodegarius, was about a mile away. By 1843 the population was large enough to justify it having it own district church. St John's was built on land given by Ichabod Wright, a Nottingham banker who lived nearby at Mapperley Hall.

Nottingham City Council

Penn Home Almshouses

This small group of almshouses was built in 1877 on the south side of Haydn Road near Mansfield Road. A plaque on the wall of the houses informs us that they were built at the expense of Maria Christian, wife of Sydney Cartwright Esq. of Penn, Staffordshire. She was born in Nottingham in 1805 and was a member of the Wright family. The engraving was made soon after the almshouses were built. They are now known as Penn Cottages but are almost hidden from view by trees.

L. Cripwell

Haydn Road, Sherwood

Haydn Road connects Mansfield Road with Nottingham Road and is about a mile long. The houses shown in the picture are on the north side and were the first with stone walls in front. The group shown are between Victoria Road and Haddon Street. They are listed for the first time in a 1907 directory. The buildings nearer to Mansfield Road included a lace factory, which was demolished about 60 years ago. The Kinema was one of the buildings erected on the cleared site.

5 Bernard Street, Carrington
The photograph was taken in 1903 outside the house of Albert Atkey. He was already a successful businessman and an early dealer in 'horseless carriages'. He is shown with his wife in one he no doubt owned, with a chauffer to drive it. He went on to have a notable career in national and local politics, becoming an MP, Lord Mayor of Nottingham in 1928 and was knighted in 1935. The first houses on Bernard Street were built in 1881 on a site on the east side of Hucknall Road.

Nottingham Historical Film Unit

Black Swan public house

The photograph was taken in 1905 shortly before the public house was demolished. It is shown on a map of 1825 as being on the east side of Mansfield turnpike road and near to what today is Woodthorpe Drive.

Mansfield Road

This illustration is a reproduction of a picture postcard for which the photograph was taken in about 1912. The viewpoint was the crest of a hill near Devon Drive, looking northwards. The Methodist Church was erected in 1884 but was demolished in 1970, with a new one built on the same site.

Nottingham City Council

Carlyle House, Ebury Road

Ebury Road connects Sherwood Rise with Hucknall Road and Carlyle House was one of the first houses to be built there in about 1889. The occupant in 1900 when the photograph was taken was Joseph Truman, a lace manufacturer. The house is still there with mature trees in its grounds. The view from the road is restricted by a large wall but the unusual window pattern on the two wings can be seen.

Daybrook Vale

This photograph is dated 1905 and shows the large house and lake in what was then a rural area on Edwards Lane. It was the home of Charles Joseph Mee, a florist with a shop on Long Row. He became a city councillor, alderman and justice of the peace.

The area was transformed in the 1920s when Valley Road was constructed and Edwards Lane made a major road. After the Mee family left, the house became a civil defence training centre. Later, the lake was filled in and the buildings demolished to form the site of houses, known as Larwood Gardens.

Nottingham City Council

L. Cripwell

Cedars Hospital

The photograph was taken in the early 1900s and shows two large houses that were joined together to make a convalescent home in 1897. Sir Charles Seely purchased the houses and gave them to the General Hospital. The site on Mansfield Road is almost opposite Albermarle Road. When the houses were built in the early 19th century they were the only buildings in the area, known as Cavendish Hill. The Cedars was used as a rehabilitation centre until recently.

L. Cripwell

Bagthorpe Infirmary

In 1836 a new body called the Board of Guardians was formed to administer the Poor Laws. These were to look after those unable to fend for themselves – orphans, aged, infirm, vagrants and in times of unemployment generally those for whom there was no work. The Nottingham Guardians built a new workhouse in 1841 on York Street. This was demolished in the 1890s when the site was needed for the Great Central Railway. A new workhouse and infirmary were built on a site on the edge of the city and after a century of social change the site now contains the City Hospital.

Bagthorpe Military Hospital

This photograph was taken during the period of World War One and shows how the Poor Law infirmary was used as a temporary military hospital for wounded soldiers. The City Council took over the Guardians responsibilities in 1931 and ran the renamed City Hospital until 1948, when it became part of the National Health Service.

Carrington Lido

In the 1930s Nottingham City Council opened three open-air swimming pools, the photo showing the one on Mansfield Road which was near St John's Church. The other two were at Highfields and Bulwell. They were called 'lidos', after the beach resort in Venice. Although popular at first when the weather was suitable, they could not compete with the Mediterranean holiday resorts in recent years. The one at Carrington was closed down a few years ago and a children's playground created on the site.

LENTON

Like other Anglo-Saxon villages near to the borough of Nottingham, Lenton was a settlement founded on the River Leen. In fact, it took its name from the river, meaning a tun or farm on the Leen. The settlements remained as small agricultural villages, as is evidenced in the *Domesday Book* of 1086 compiled by the Norman invasion of England. However, Lenton was to undergo a change in the 12th century when a Cluniac priory was established. This became the most powerful of the religious houses in the county, due to the granting by wealthy Normans of land which provided the priory with sustenance.

This came to end in the 16th century when the king ordered the dissolution of all these religious houses and the priory buildings were demolished. Lenton continued to be a parish as did the other settlements, which remained agricultural villages. From the mid-17th century onwards, the East Midlands became a centre for the domestic industry making hosiery in the homes on stocking frames.

Nottingham and the villages benefitted from this, as is shown in the figures of population in the 1801 census. Nottingham had tripled its population in 30 years and Lenton had grown to 893. The census also showed the size of the parishes, Lenton being by far the largest at 5,080 acres. All the villages and the borough continued to grow in population and size as industrial centres, especially in lace manufacture. In Lenton's case this resulted in the establishment of a new settlement nearer to the borough, called New Lenton. As a result of the increased industry and populations, Nottingham obtained an Extension Act in 1877, which brought the five former villages into the borough. While the effect was to unify them in due course, Lenton benefitted straightaway by the action of the borough in construction of an outer ring of boulevards which aided communications. Two of these were of direct benefit to Lenton, one of which was the building of a low level road later named Castle Boulevard which made it easier for horse traffic that up to then had to use the steep hill of Derby Road. The other three boulevards, Lenton, Radford and Gregory, formed with Castle Boulevard three sides of a square, which helped travel and communication between Lenton and the adjoining areas.

In the last quarter of the 19th century the enlarged borough, which became a city in 1897, witnessed a growing diversification of industry to complement its worldwide lace trade. Lenton shared this trend with the setting up in its boundaries of the Raleigh Cycle Company. This in turn was accompanied by the building of a large number of new houses in a part of Lenton known as Lenton Sands.

After World War One Nottingham was faced with a number of problems arising from ageing and unfit houses and lack of modern facilities. It was to tackle this in a limited way of demolition of older houses. Nottingham was also embarking on a major project – erecting council houses. Some of these were put up in Lenton, and a more widespread alteration of the undeveloped land to the south west. The major event was the development of the Highfields site, with the erection of the University College, a public park and an open-air swimming pool and the building of a new major road, University Boulevard.

In the post-1945 era Lenton again saw major changes. The building of a new bridge over the River Trent enabled a new industrial site to be built on Lenton Lane, after controlled tipping was stabilised and a new section of the A52 was diverted along it to form part of an outer ring road. Demolition of most of the 19th-century smaller houses paved the way for the erection of five multi-storey blocks of flats in the Willoughby Street area.

Later, the building of the University Teaching Hospital, the Queen's Medical Centre and of the Jubilee Campus were major events, as was, on the other hand, the loss of the Raleigh Cycle factories.

The photographs show how the older Lenton has been transformed in the 20th century.

Lenton Railway Station

The first railway line in Nottingham was from Derby and was part of the Midland Counties Railway. The line ran from Carrington Street westwards to Derby and in 1848 a branch line was added at Lenton North Junction near Derby Road. The first station was at Lenton and was in use until the discontinuance of many lines in the 1960s. The station could be seen from Church Street bridge until a few years ago, it has since been demolished. The line is now part of the Robin Hood Line.

Holy Trinity Church

The population of Lenton had increased so much by 1840 that the old Priory Church was inadequate and was in a poor state of repair. In 1842 a new church was designed by H.I. Stevens and built on a site near to what is today Lenton Boulevard. The engraving shows the school and the teacher's house alongside the church. The engraving was by a London firm, Rock Brothers.

Holy Trinity Church

This view of the church is reproduced from a picture postcard of the 1900s. It shows a different view from that of the engraving above. The picture would have been from a photograph and this shows that the engraving was accurate.

White Hart Inn, Gregory Street

This drawing shows the garden at the rear of the inn and was reproduced from a book published in 1926 of 50 drawings by Thomas William Hammond. Born in the United States in 1854, he came to live in Nottingham at the age of four. He became a skilled designer of lace curtains but is better known as a recorder of scenes in Nottingham, which he creates in pencil sketches and charcoal. The White Hart Inn included a part used as the Peveril Prison for Debtors.

Abbey Street

This small group of houses was photographed on 12 March 1913 by an inspector of Nottingham City Council. They had been built about a 100 years before when the population of Lenton started to grow. The long windows on the second floor were designed to give light for some of the complicated operations on the stocking frames, which were worked mainly by men in their homes.

Abbey Street

This photograph was taken three years after the previous picture and shows how the houses had been altered to two storeys instead of three, and how one of them had been converted into a shop. Clarke's clothing shop is on the right of both pictures.

Abbey Square, Abbey Street

The photograph shows three sides of a square and the two dwellings at the rear are Nos 5 and 7. There were six houses altogether. Abbey Square was off Abbey Street, near to Gregory Street. The houses are quite attractive in appearance but the interiors and amenities were far from modern standards. They were among the first dwellings to be demolished when slum clearance started.

Nottingham City Council

Choral Yard, Abbey Street
This photograph was taken on 12 May 1915 and shows Nos 3 and 4 Choral Yard. This was one of several yards off Abbey Street on the west side near Gregory Street, the others being Abbey Square and Priory Square.

The houses look as though they were rather more elegant than most of the older dwellings.

Nottingham City Council

Lenton House
The photograph was taken about a 100 years ago and the house had been built on land which was sold by auction in 1797. Its first occupier was Matthew Needham, a surgeon. Several similar large houses were built about the same time on land to the west of the village. They became attractive to the wealthy Nottingham resident who wished to get away from the increasingly industrialised town. They now provide accommodation for the University of Nottingham.

16 Park Street

Park Street was one of the new streets in New Lenton, as the growing population needed an area nearer to Nottingham than the old village. This street was off Derby Road and ran parallel to Willoughby Street. The street and the houses disappeared when the clearance of the whole area took place in the 1960s. The statue on the wall was of Jonas Hanway, the first person in England to carry an umbrella. It seems to have been used to call attention to its role as an antiques shop.

Albert Ball Memorial Homes

These almshouses were founded to commemorate Captain Albert Ball, VC, one of the RFC fighter pilots killed in World War One. He was only 18 when he was shot down. His father, also Albert, was a member of the Ball family who had lived in Lenton for many years. He was a prominent businessman in Nottingham and was a member of the City Council, becoming an alderman and mayor on two occasions and later Lord Mayor. He was also chairman of the Nottingham Corporation Gas Committee.

Lenton War Memorial

The photograph was taken at the opening of the World War One memorial. It stood on a piece of land at the junction of Church Street and Sherwin Street and had been paid for by subscriptions from residents. Nearly 200 men and women from Lenton had been killed in the war and plaques on three sides list their names. The front plaque lists the officers and sergeants, while those on the two sides give the names of corporals and other ranks. The rear plaque gives the abbreviations used for the various units.

NEW BASFORD

As mentioned in an earlier chapter, as Old Basford became overcrowded with an increased population due to the growth of the textile trades, new settlements arose at Carrington and Hyson Green. A little earlier, the first houses in New Basford were built on land that had been sold in 1814. This was to the south of Old Basford, about a mile away near the parish boundary. The new suburb grew quickly, mainly due to the expiry of Heathcoat's patent lace-making machine. Men were able to make or buy similar machines in what became known as 'bobbinet fever'. Despite changes in fashions and economic fluctuations, the lace trade, which was to become Nottingham's leading industry, continued to grow. New Basford played a prominent part in this, due in some extent to two enterprising lace manufacturers in partnership, Biddle and Birkin. They both later moved their growing businesses to Nottingham and both became aldermen on the Borough Council.

New Basford continued to grow and in the 10 years between 1841 to 1851 its population doubled to 2,343. Lace and hosiery were beginning to be made on larger steam-powered machines in factories. Another large industry was Shipstone's Brewery. After 1877 when Basford became part of the Borough of Nottingham, New Basford and adjoining parts of Radford at Hyson Green were to benefit from the construction of a new through road from Nottingham to Bulwell, called Radford Road. This enabled easier transport of goods, and in the early years of the 20th century of passengers on trams and later trolley buses and omnibuses.

On the eastern side of New Basford, Nottingham Road played a similar part in connecting the town with Old and New Basford. These developments helped to extend the area of New Basford in the late 19th century and early 20th century. The area to the north of the original settlement around North Gate and Mount Street was built up as far as Fairfax Street, with streets connecting Radford Road and Nottingham Road. A similar situation arose in the south-east corner of New Basford with development on both sides of Nottingham. Another important development was the building of the Corporation's Gas Works.

The lace and engineering industries continued to expand with large factories, some of which are still there but used for other purposes. The earliest houses built were, of course, growing older all the time, a situation not helped by the two world wars. In 1960 Nottingham City Council obtained a compulsory purchase order for an area bounded by North Gate, Rawson Street, Beech Avenue and High Church Street. Most of the houses had been represented as unfit, but a small number of fit houses were included to permit better redevelopment. A number of other buildings were included, again to allow a properly planned redevelopment. These included shops, public houses, a chapel, a Salvation Army Hall, a brewery and a pickle factory.

Once the houses and buildings had been demolished, the council did not build new council houses but created a new street layout and leased land for new, lighter industries. Some of the older industrial buildings were no longer viable for such use and were either converted or demolished. Much of the rest of the enlarged New Basford area remains unchanged.

Nottingham City Council

St Augustine's Church

New Basford in its early years was part of the ecclesiastical parish church of St Leodegarius. As it was not a long journey from New Basford, there was at first no move for it to have its own church. This was partly due to the fact that many of the residents preferred the Methodist Church. *Wright's Directory* of 1853 listed three Methodist and two Baptist churches. In 1848 a new benefactor for New Basford had the Reverend Thomas Bolton as first incumbent. The first services were held in a building in Olive Square. Reverend Mr Bolton was mainly responsible for the building of a new St Augustine's Church, paying for much of it himself.

Nottingham City Council

Nottingham Road

This photograph has been dated as 3 July 1937 and was of the official opening of Chelsea Baptist Chapel. This was to replace the former chapel on Chelsea Street. The new building is still in use, at the junction of Haydn Road.

George L. Roberts

Rawson Street

The building on the right was a Methodist Church in 1964 when the photograph was taken but it has since been extended and converted into an Indian Community Centre. The street leading off Rawson Street is Mosley Street and the shop on the corner has been demolished.

North Gate and Suez Street

Nos 1 to 7 are on Suez Street on the left of the picture taken in 1954. Those on the right are 110 to 120 North Gate. The photograph shows the rear of the houses and the drying ground/childrens' playground. These were the only houses on the north side of the clearance area beyond North Gate.

Osberton Street

This photograph was taken about 1965 when most of the houses in the 1960 New Basford Clearance Area had been demolished. Osberton Street was a short street 20 yards long and had seven houses.

It connected Chelsea Street with Palm Street and the photograph shows the view looking westwards. Shipstone's Brewery's tower can be seen on the left between two chimneys. The street has been built on since.

Nottingham Historical Film Unit

Signal box near Haydn Road

The Great Central Railway, later the London and North Eastern Railway, came to Nottingham Victoria Station by 1965. It entered the city at Bulwell with a station at Bulwell Common, and another two at Haydn Road (New Basford Station) and Carrington before entering a tunnel to Victoria Station. The whole line closed in the 1960s; the Station House still exists on Haydn Road.

G.D. Christian

Nottingham Road

The first trolley buses to run in Nottingham were from Nottingham via Mansfield Road and Sherwood Rise to Basford. The last ones were in 1966 and the picture shows two of them at the Basford terminus near Valley Road. The Futurist cinema can be seen behind the buses and the former Westminster Bank can be seen partly on Valley Road.

Copyright: Nottingham Evening Post

Lace factory, Chelsea Street

The photograph, taken in 1972, is of a lace factory of J. Jardine Limited, shortly before it was demolished. It shows the huge size of lace machines, which had developed from the stocking frames. J. Jardine Limited also made Petite typewriters in part of the factory. John Jardine was born in Hull in 1825 and came to Nottingham when he was nine. He was described as a unique mechanical genius who founded the business of lace machine manufacture. He died in 1895, leaving a considerable estate of £50,581.

New Basford Council School

The building on Radford Road was opened in November 1877. It was part of the building of schools by the Nottingham School Board, an elected body. It became New Basford Council School when the board was discontinued in 1902, when education was transferred to the City Council. The plaque with the name of the school can be seen in the picture taken in 1973. The school has since been replaced by North Gate Primary School on Suez Street and the plaque can now be seen in the grounds behind a fence on Eland Street.

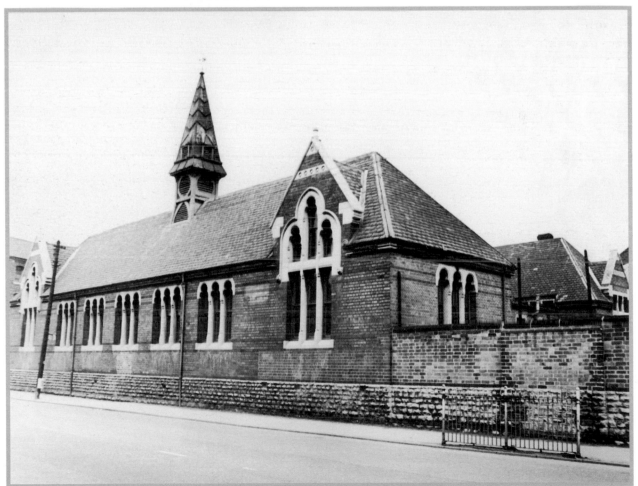

Reg Baker

Reg Baker

New Basford Church of England School

A number of Nottingham's schools in the 19th century were established by the Church of England. The photograph, taken in 1975, is of the one started in New Basford by St Augustine's Church on High Church Street. Like the church itself, its creation was due in a large measure to the vicar, the Reverend Thomas Bolton.

Reg Baker

Shipstone Terrace

Shipstone Terrace was a small terrace on the south side of Shipstone Street. The name Shipstone was given because of its nearness to Shipstone's Brewery. The whole terrace was demolished in the 1970s, as were the houses on the right of the picture. The cleared site has been made into a children's playground, which is just a few feet away from the Shipstone Street tram stop.

Ekowe Terrace

Ekowe Street was one of the later developments of New Basford, north of North Gate. Ekowe Terrace was on the east side of Ekowe Street in 1976. The houses have since been demolished and two pairs of houses erected on the site.

Regent Street

This photograph taken in 1976 shows Regent Street, which runs eastwards from Gawthorne Street. It does not connect directly with Nottingham Road. The buildings just visible at the end of the street were part of John Player's depot, in the former Thomas Adams's factory. The buildings have since been demolished and the Djanogly College built on the site.

BOBBERS MILL AND HYSON GREEN

These two districts adjoin each other but have quite different histories. Bobbers Mill was wholly in Radford parish, but Hyson Green was partly in Radford parish and partly in Lenton up to the end of the 19th century.

Bobbers Mill was mentioned in writing in 1335, and on a map of 1609 it is shown as a mill over the River Leen and is named Bavers Mill. In *White's Directory* of 1832 it is described as an ancient corn mill which gives its name to a new village, where there are two bleach works and a Kilhamite and Wesleyan Chapel. Some 16 years later a railway line on the Midland Counties Railway from Nottingham northwards passed through Bobbers Mill with the convenience of a level crossing, which continued to delay traffic for nearly a 100 years. It ceased to function in 1931 when a new road bridge was built. This was followed by road improvements to Nuthall Road and Aspley Lane and the building of modern houses. A few of the 19th-century houses still remain on Cyril and Albert Avenues but the rest of the area is mainly industrial. The Wheatsheaf public house was mentioned in *White's Directory* of 1832.

The directory gives a fuller account of Hyson Green, which it describes it as 'another well-built village which has been built in the last 10 years and is said to have had its name from the tea gardens, to which parties frequently resorted after a summer's walk, to quench their thirst with hyson and other nectarous draughts'.

It stated that the population then was about 2,000 people and the houses were built on the north side of what is today Gregory Boulevard, with new streets on each side of what was then Basford Road, becoming Radford Road later. Pleasant Row was one of the earliest streets to be laid out and maps show that they had long rear gardens. The houses had been built as a kind of working men's club, similar to that at Carrington. These were all the result of the spread of early lace manufacture in what was known as 'bobbinet fever'.

Both Bobbers Mill and Hyson Green continued to grow throughout the 19th century and to become part of the development of Radford parish. The Borough Extension Act of 1877 brought Radford, Lenton and Basford into the borough, which eventually resulted in their becoming more closely integrated.

A. McArthur

Bobbers Mill

This is a reproduction of a painting dated about 1890 by an artist A. McArthur. Even allowing for a certain amount of artistic licence it showed what a rural place Bobbers Mill was at that time. There is still a public house called The Wheatsheaf on the same site, but it is a more modern building. Today the 1930s bridge starts a little to the right of the public house.

Nottingham City Council

Mosley's Buildings

These small houses on Plantation Side are shown on an ordnance survey map of 1913. The site was used in the 1920s for the construction of Darley Avenue. The large archway was probably the entrance to a farm for wagons loaded with hay. The photograph is believed to have been taken about 1880.

Nottingham Historical Film Unit

Bobbers Mill

This photograph taken in 1906 is of the mill on the River Leen, which gave its name to that part of Radford on which it stands. It is mentioned in writing as early as the 14th century when it was called Boberismilne, no doubt after the name of its owner. The sluice where the water came back after the mill had used it can be seen on the right.

Bobbers Mill

This shows the mill in 1930, 24 years after the previous scene. It shows how the River Leen had been widened to provide a good head of water. An ordnance survey map of 1913 shows a small branch line from the adjoining railway to the mill. The River Leen was subsequently culverted and the site used for industrial concerns.

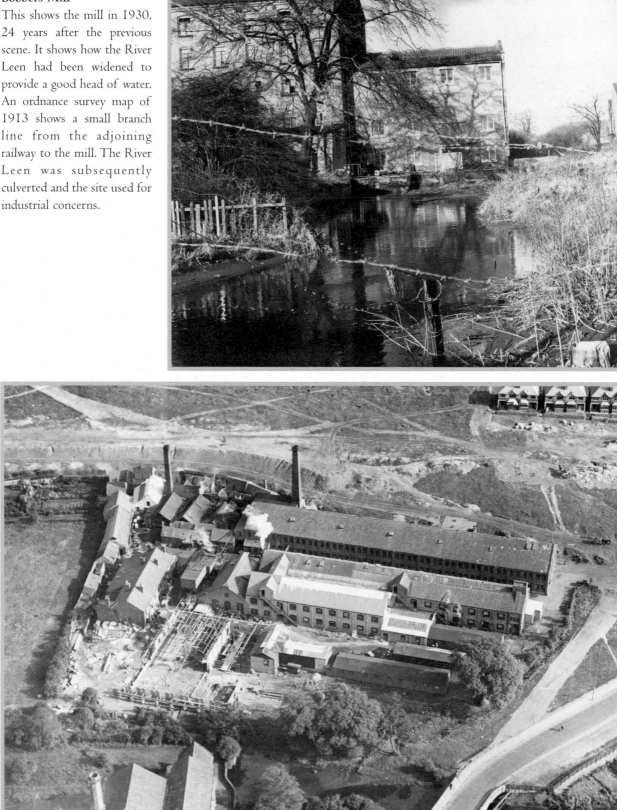

Copyright: Nottingham Evening Post

Nottingham City Council

Bobbers Mill

This photograph shows how the land between the railway line and Plantation Side had become an industrial site by 1927. The main buildings were those of Lindley and Lindley's bleach works, dating from about 1892.

Nottingham City Council

Level crossing, Bobbers Mill

This picture was taken in 1931 when the new bridge over the railway can be seen on the right. It was not then open to traffic and the level crossing was still in use. The road was the original road through Bobbers Mill to Basford. After the new bridge came into use the level crossing was closed with a pedestrian footbridge over the railway. A short stretch of the road still exists on the other side of the railway.

Grand Theatre

The Grand Theatre opened in 1886 and is situated on the west side of Radford Road between a cul-de-sac, Bright Row and Gregory Boulevard. It presented plays including some by Shakespeare and was visited on many occasions by the D'Oyle Carte Opera Company performing Gilbert and Sullivan's works. It had a more chequered career in the early 20th century with drama, variety and early silent films. It became solely a cinema in the 1930s until it closed in 1956.

A.P. Knighton

Nottingham City Council

Pleasant Row

On the west side of Radford Road, just north of Gregory Boulevard, was Pleasant Row. Those houses in the picture were in one of several terraces on the north side of the row, probably Thornton or Anson Terraces. The houses of which the backs can be seen were on St Paul's Avenue. Pleasant Court, a new block of council dwellings, was built on the sites of Pleasant Row and the terraces in the 1960s.

L. Cripwell

The Old General public house

The photograph is said to be about 1912 and although the public house still exists at the junction of Radford Road and Bobbers Mill Road, its appearance is different now. It does, however, have the effigy on the Bobbers Mill Road flank of Benjamin Mayo. He was a somewhat eccentric character given the pseudonym The Old General from his custom on ceremonial occasions of marching ahead of children playing a tin whistle. He died in 1843.

Nottingham City Council

St Luke's Church

This 'iron' church was erected in 1883 to meet the needs of growth of population in Hyson Green, which had only one Church of England at the time, St Paul's. It was only temporary, as the site on which it was built had been acquired for a new permanent church. The 'iron' church was built 80 yards from Bobbers Mill Road. Its name was later changed to St Simon's to avoid confusion with St Luke's Church on Carlton Road. St Simon's was demolished soon after the new St Stephen's Church was built nearer to the road.

St Stephen's Church

The illustration appeared in *The Builder* on 2 October 1897. It shows the proposed new church on Bobbers Mill Road and was drawn by the architect W.D. Caröe FRIBA. This was for a new permanent church for a new parish, St Stephen's, to replace a temporary 'iron' church named St Simon's (see picture above). The new church was given the same name as the one which was demolished as part of the site for Victoria Station.

EXTERIOR.
CHURCH OF ST. STEPHEN, NOTTINGHAM.—Mr. W. D. Caröe, F.R.I.B.A., Architect.

Nottingham City Council

Scotholme Council School

This building on Beaconsfield Street and Carver Street was built in 1880 and enlarged in 1883 with accommodation for 852 children. In the 1920s the Education Committee used part of the school as a clinic for children requiring spectacles, dentistry and minor illnesses, for those whose parents could not afford doctors' fees. The need for such clinics finished when the National Health Service started in 1948. The buildings are now used as a cultural centre for the association of Caribbean residents and friends. The appearance of the buildings is little changed today from that in 1973 when the photograph was taken.

Reg Baker

Forest Recreation Ground

This aerial photograph was taken about 1927. The road in the centre of the picture is Gregory Boulevard going eastwards. The open space on the left was later used for the erection of the Manning School for girls, opened in 1931 and recently demolished. A new Djanogly College has been built on the site. Noel Street is at the bottom of the picture and the houses in the bottom left-hand corner were demolished under the Hyson Green clearance scheme.

Nottingham City Council

Copyright: *Nottingham Evening Post*

Ewart Road

In 1883 Thomas Isaac Birkin (later Sir Thomas, Baronet) submitted a plan for building houses on what he called the Forest Ville Estate. This was to be on land east of Noel Street to Sherwood Rise and north of the new Gregory Boulevard to Gladstone Street. The street plan was on the grid pattern with straight streets at right angles to each other. It was to be a completely residential area and most of the earliest houses were large expensive ones. About 1,905 smaller houses without forecourts were built on new streets. One of these was Ewart Road, from Gladstone Street to Laurie Avenue. By 1910 it was fully built up with 150 houses.

The photograph taken in 1953 shows celebrations for the Queen's Coronation and the Victorian cobblestones still formed the surface of the street.

Gregory Boulevard

This photograph was taken about 1897 from Nottingham Forest. It shows the boulevard and some of the earliest houses starting at the Mansfield Road end. The house on the left of the picture, with two gables, is Foxhall Lodge, at the corner of Foxhall Road. There were eight other larger houses to the right. All were occupied in 1899 by owners of city businesses: an alderman John Barber, a former mayor of Nottingham, the general manager of the Raleigh Cycle Company and a girls' boarding school. The wooden post separated the boulevard from the Forest racecourse.

J. Buist

RADFORD

The original settlements of Radford and Lenton both took their names from the River Leen. Their parish churches were just a mile apart. As explained in the chapter on Lenton, the latter grew in size when the Cluniac Priory was there. In the census figures of 1801 Lenton, with 5,080 acres, had a population of 893, while Radford, with 1,000 acres, had 2,269. This growth in population was described in *White's Directory* of 1832, which stated that Radford 'has drank so deeply of the manufacturing spirit of Nottingham that it now ranks as the second most populous parish in the county'. Its population in 1831 was 9,806 and 1,100 new houses had been built in the previous 10 years. The directory listed the names of 285 bobbinet makers. The population grew to nearly 17,000 by 1877, when Radford along with the other adjoining parishes became part of the borough. By this time much of the lace and hosiery industries was concentrated in steam-powered factories.

The parish had to pay a heavy price for this growth in the limited area available. This was reflected in two scathing reports by the Privy Council after the area had been inspected because of the outbreaks of diseases. The report drew attention to the overcrowding, lack of sanitation and polluted water supplies. It also criticised the district for not having a Board of Health or a Medical Officer of Health. This was remedied for a few years until the parish became part of the borough.

An important part of the transfer was that Radford had to submit all proposals for new buildings to the council for approval, as did all parts of the extended borough. The council made sure that all new houses were built to a better standard with proper sanitation. The last quarter of the 19th century saw Radford's population increase to 35,000 and many of the new houses built in that period are still there today.

However, little was done in general to remedy the defects of the older houses, not only in the borough but also in the other former parishes, until January 1909. The City Council then decided to have a Housing Committee and the first meeting took place on the 11 January, and on the 9 February the committee members met at the junction of Forest Road and Alfreton Road to see insanitary houses, including some on Parker Street. Their powers were limited but at least something was being done.

This was halted after World War One. From 1920 to 1939 was a period of progress, which included the building of council houses and the start of clearing large areas of insanitary houses. Yet, again war prevented further progress and it was not until 1954 that a resumption of clearance could begin again. The first major scheme was at Radford under the name of Denman Street, the spine of an area bounded by Canning Circus, Hartley Road, Alfreton Road and Ilkeston Road. Most of the older houses were demolished and the sites used for building high-rise and other flats and maisonettes.

Nottingham City Council

St Peter's Street

This photograph is thought to have been taken in the late 1800s. The building was erected by the Radford Board of Guardians in 1838 as a workhouse to replace the old parish building. When Radford became part of the borough in 1877, it continued to be used until the borough built a new one for the whole city at Bagthorpe. It was then used as an ordinary house until it was demolished as part of a clearance area.

Nottingham City Council

The White Horse, Ilkeston Road

The photograph of this public house was taken in the early 1900s. The street sign on the left shows that it was opposite the end of St Peter's Street, which reveals how narrow Ilkeston Road was then. The road was widened and the White Horse rebuilt along with the adjoining houses. The public house there still retains the same name, but all the buildings around have been built recently.

Radford Boulevard Council School

The picture on a postcard shows the school on Ilkeston Road and Radford Boulevard. As it also shows a tram it was probably taken in the early 20th century. The school was built for the Nottingham School Board and opened in 1886. After it was enlarged in 1894, it could accommodate 1,101 pupils. Its three departments meant that they could have all their education in the same building from five years to 13, later increased to 14. The building is still there but used for other educational purposes.

A.P. Knighton

This shop has the name F. Mitchell on the window of the motor and cycle depot. He was Frederick Mitchell. The photograph was dated 1900 soon after he became the occupier. By 1904 he had moved to Alfreton Road. He later became one of the leading motorcar dealers in the city. He also played a prominent part in public affairs, becoming an alderman and in 1943 was Lord Mayor of Nottingham. Frederick Mitchell was also involved in the development of Beeston Fields Golf Club.

This photograph is said to be of the wife of Frederick Mitchell. Was she a bicycle rider or acting as a model for her husband's business?

Nottingham City Council

Bainbridges Yard

This photograph is precisely dated 8 November 1912 and was no doubt taken by the Health Department. It does appear in the 1910 directory but not thereafter, so it was probably demolished shortly after the photograph was taken. The yard was off Moorgate Street which was parallel to Alfreton Road near to Wood Street, both of which are still there.

Nottingham City Council

Montfort Street

This photograph was probably taken for the same reason as the previous one. It is dated 8 September 1913 and gives the houses numbered 1, 3, 5 and 7. Only house numbered 1 of them appeared in a 1910 directory but all had gone in later directories.

Montfort Street was a small street that ran from Ilkeston Road past Greek Square to Denman Street and part is still there.

Nottingham City Council

Bostocks Yard

This single house in a yard off St Peter's Street was photographed on 24 July 1915, almost certainly by the Health Department. Despite the outbreak of war in 1914, it seems that the department were still able to inspect houses with a view to demolition or to be used other than living in, as a store for instance. The occupants seem to be unaware that putting a horseshoe upside down brought back luck.

Alfreton Road

This view is recorded as being pre-1930s. The general appearance seems to be of the left-hand side of Alfreton Road below Hartley Road. The 1932 directory gives No. 381 as a tobacconists, 383 a grocers, then Beckenham Road, then five more houses or shops and finally Player's tobacco factory. All these seem to fit the picture.

A.P. Knighton

A.P. Knighton

Old Radford Church
The photograph suggests a date between 1900 and 1920 and as it has number 25 on it, this would perhaps mean it was a picture postcard.

Nottingham City Council

Aerial view, Radford Boulevard
This excellent aerial view, taken some 70 years ago by Surrey Flying Services, is described as John Player and Sons Tobacco Factory. This is shown clearly in the centre of the picture. Equally clearly is Alfreton Road, shown on the left.

Montfort Street
This photograph, taken in 1955, shows Montfort Street after the houses on it had been demolished. It was a short street from Ilkeston Road to the south end of Denman Street. The right-hand shop in the picture was at the corner of Burke Street and Frederick Spencer was the occupier. The advertisement on the wall for Tenants Rock Ales was for the Phoenix public house.

Warner Street
This view of Warner Street was taken from Garfield Street looking towards Radford Boulevard. The two blocks of houses differ in style and were probably built by different builders.

Stilton Terrace
This small terrace of houses was off Norton Street between Hartley Road and Beckenham Road. The site was used, along with that of other demolished properties, for building Norton Court.

Norton Street
The building in the photograph was taken shortly before its demolition in about 1960. Together with its adjoining building in Hartley Road it was erected in the 1890s by the Nottingham Union, which was responsible for the care of orphaned and other children without proper guardianship. This duty was transferred to the City Council in 1929 when the union was dissolved. The buildings then became known as the Scattered Homes and after the Children Act 1948 they became offices for the Children's Department.

Cobden Street

A small estate of houses and shops was built in the 1870s between Lenton Boulevard and Faraday Road. Cobden Street, shown here in the photograph, was one of these. It ran southwards from Ilkeston Road but stopped short a few yards further south. Ilkeston Road was reached along Guthrie Street on the right while on the left is Salisbury Street, which ran as far as Faraday Road.

Salisbury Street

Taken in 1976, this view was from the junction of Bright Street looking westwards to Faraday Road. A faint glimpse of the gasometer of Radford Gasworks can be seen beyond Faraday Road. Sixty-nine Salisbury Street was the Variety Club. Most of the houses have been demolished, although a public house, the Marquis of Lorne. still stands on the north side of the street.

Dulwich Road

A small group of streets between St Peters Street and Hartley Road have names of London districts. In addition to Dulwich Road, there are Croydon, Norwood, Brixton and Sydenham Roads. Dulwich Road ran from Denman Street to Norwood Road.

Christ Church

This church, erected in 1847 on Ilkeston Road, between Ronald Street and Baldwin Street, was demolished in 1950 and the site made into a pleasant garden.

Caulton Street

This street runs from Alfreton Road, the first street on the right-hand side past Bentinck Road. It connected to Radford Road. The first mention of it is in a directory of 1885. The width of the street and the standard of the houses contrast with the narrow streets and small houses of the earlier-built parts of Radford.

Radford Woodhouse

This part of Radford was detached from the main part of Old Radford and owed its existence to the nearby Nottingham Canal. There was also a wharf where Thomas North built a mineral railway line to load coal on to barges. The photograph is dated September 1927 when it was still fairly rural.

Radford Woodhouse

This pair of houses stood near a lock on the Nottingham Canal near to Ilkeston Road. They were probably built early in the 19th century.

Vane Street

There were three short streets which led off the east side of Radford Bridge Road: Vane Street in the photograph, Gates Street and Leavers Street. They were all cul-de-sacs and in the 1960s they were all demolished.

SNEINTON

Like Nottingham itself, Sneinton took its name from a tribal leader. Apparently, the Normans could not pronounce the initial letter 's' but its neighbours, the Anglo Saxons, could. Chapman's map of 1774 showed that the heart of the original settlement was still about a quarter of a mile from its border with Nottingham. Sixty years later, Sanderson's map showed that a New Sneinton had grown up nearer the town where Bath Street is today. This was the consequence of its population increase from 558 in 1801 to 3,605 30 years later. It had grown due to the same industrial expansion that had resulted in the town's even greater expansion.

This was to continue until 1877, when Sneinton became part of the Borough under an Extension Act that brought other adjoining parishes in as well. Sneinton was the smallest of them at 911 acres. Despite this, it grew to a population of 23,000 by 1901. This was almost the same as Lenton, which had 5,000 acres.

Sneinton's growth was limited by its physical layout. Its border with Nottingham on the north side stretched as far as the border with Carlton and on the south it bordered on the River Trent. Growth southwards was also limited due to railways. Nevertheless, the 20th century saw considerable extension along Sneinton Dale and Colwick Road, with council houses in the part of Sneinton Dale on the far side of the suburban railway line. The wooded slope from Colwick Road northwards did provide a pleasant green fringe with extensive views over the Trent Valley.

The increasing age of the houses built in the first half of the 19th century meant that Sneinton was one of the first areas to receive clearance orders. Part of the redevelopment included multi-storey flats. Today, much of the early 20th-century housing remains in reasonable condition and Sneinton has become a popular residential area, partly due to its nearness to the city's shops and other attractions.

Nottingham City Council

Sneinton Hermitage
This is a reproduction of another of Thomas Hammond's drawings, done in 1888. The White Swan Inn is the building on the left and next door is a wall of the Earl Manvers public house. The two houses were numbered 3 and 5 Sneinton Hermitage in a directory.

32 Walker Street

Walker Street was one of a number of streets which formed a group between Carlton Road and Windmill Lane, and from Dakeyne Street to Sneinton Road. In this photograph, said to have been taken in the 1880s, No. 32 was where Robert Millhouse, a stocking maker and poet, died in 1839. There appears to be a memorial plaque over the door.

Lord Nelson public house

Known colloquially as The White House, the public house on Thurgarton Street is still there. When this photograph was taken about 1898, the landlord was John Bamforth. At that time there were only one or two streets beyond it.

Belvoir Hill

Belvoir Hill was at the top of a short hill off Dale Street and had a number of large houses built in Regency style. At the rear can be seen Sneinton Windmill, now restored and the home at the time of George Green, whose mathematical talents have been recognised in recent years.

Windmill Lane

This view is taken from the southern end on Sneinton Road. The house on the right-hand corner of the photograph was the vicarage.

T. Wallis Gordon

Hermitage Square

This photograph was taken about 1910 by T. Wallis Gordon, who was then the Deputy City Engineer. The two streets on the left appear to be St Stephens Road and Sneinton Hollows, and the view to the right is Thurgarton Street.

Ann Day

Colwick Road

This view was taken not very far away from the picture above. Meadow Lane is on the right and the tram is on Colwick Road. John Whiting's pawnbrokers shop is at the junction of Colwick Road and Sneinton Boulevard. The date is about 1907.

George L. Roberts

Windmill Lane

This photograph was taken about 1912 and is said to be of houses on the north side. They were probably nearby the present Queen Adelaide public house.

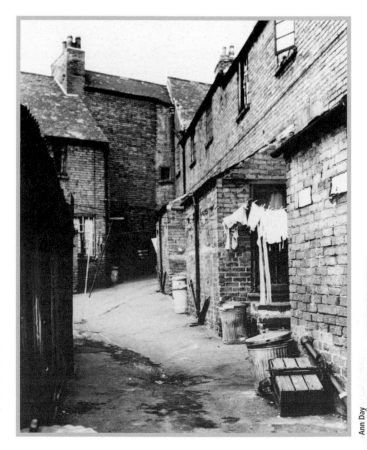

Eldon Street

Taken in 1956 just before the clearance scheme started, the rear of the houses on the right were of Nos 1–7 Kingston Street. The other houses were on Lower Eldon Street, on the south side of Sneinton Road.

Ann Day

Eldon Street

This view is of Upper Eldon Street, which is on the north side of Sneinton Road and leads on to Walker Street. Taken in 1958, the photograph shows the stone wall of one of the new houses built on ground which had been cleared of houses earlier.

98 Sneinton Road

This was one of 14 receiving offices of the National Laundry in the city. In the days before laundrettes, laundry could be handed in at one of these offices and laundered at the works near Wilford Toll Bridge. The cleaned articles were later collected from the receiving office. Ninety-eight Sneinton Road was on the south side just above Lower Eldon Street. Boot scrapers can be seen either side of the house. Taken in about 1930, a notice in the window refers to a National Economy.

Nottingham City Council

96-108 Manvers Street
These were the only houses on the west side of Manvers Street, between Evelyn Street and the Sir Robert Peel public house. They were still there in a 1956 directory but were later demolished. The various outbuildings are shown on the next picture.

Nottingham City Council

Rear of 102–108 Manvers Street
The chimneys shown here were probably from the washhouses with a coal-fired copper.

George L. Roberts

Manvers Street

This photograph shows houses and shops on the east side of the street between Eyre Street and Pierrepont Street. The Crystal Palace public house and Newark Street were to the right of the last house in the picture. The overhead wires were for the trolley buses.

Nottingham City Council

Sneinton Dale

This photograph is thought to have been taken in the 1920s. The villas on the left were built in the early 1880s and the rest of the dale was gradually built up with houses and shops. Those on the left extended as far as the railway line and bridge by 1930. The buildings on the right-hand side stretched as far as Shrewsbury Road by that date, with the Dale Cinema and other properties in the late 1930s. Colwick Woods can just be made out further away.

Hermitage Square

This photograph was taken about 50 years later than the one on page 65. It was taken from a point further away than the previous one and shows the corner of Thurgarton Street with the former Methodist Church. On this picture it had already ceased to be used as a church. The Bendigo public house was fairly new then.

Sneinton Road

This photograph was taken in 1948 and at that time Sneinton had not changed much since the 1920s. The Post Office at the junction with Windmill Lane was demolished along with the adjoining houses and the site is now part of the Salvation Army Centre.

Sneinton Elements

This small part of Sneinton was somewhat distant when it was first built in the early 19th century. It was scheduled for redevelopment in 1939 but this was postponed because of the war. Because of its poor condition, permission was granted by the government for clearance to begin in 1952 before the main campaign began. Chedworth Close was a small new council estate built on the site.

Walker Street

The area between Sneinton Road and Walker Street was another of the older parts of Sneinton where some houses had been demolished before 1939. It was one of the first areas to be treated when in 1954, clearance areas went ahead.

This shows a part clearance taken from North Street showing the rear of houses on Bond Street. The roof of St Alban's Church can be seen in the background.

Bond Street and Haywood Street
This was taken when many of the houses in the Walker Street area had been demolished. The derelict house was on Bond Street and the public house next door was the Cricketers Rest, at the corner of North Street and Haywood Street.

Lees Hill Footway
After the main Sneinton clearance scheme was completed, a number of small schemes were implemented. Lees Hill, a short steep hill, was one of these. It linked Manvers Street with St Stephen's Road.

Thoresby Avenue
This is a picture of a short street which stretched from Meadow Lane to Sneinton Hermitage, and the rears of some of the houses. All the houses on Thoresby Avenue were demolished. The street still remains.

St Stephen's Avenue
This was another of the later small clearance areas, off St Stephen's Road.

THE MEADOWS

When the Anglo-Saxons founded a settlement on the cliff top that today houses St Mary's Church and the Lace Market, they also claimed sufficient land to the north and south to provide for the growing of food and keeping of cattle. Those lands later became common lands for the burgesses who had rights in them. This became a serious threat to the growth and development of the borough in the latter part of the 18th century because the burgesses refused to allow building on these fields, one of which was the Meadows, which stretched from the borough as far as the River Trent.

After a political struggle, which lasted 50 years, the borough council in 1845 obtained an Enclosure Act of Parliament. This provided compensation to the burgesses for their loss of rights. It also provided that an independent body of Enclosure Commissions had to be set up to re-allocate ownership of lands and to draw up plans as to how and where new building was to take place. This took some 20 years to complete. An important condition affecting the Meadows was that land should be left for public access. This was achieved by creating Queen's Walk for pedestrians and allocating land for a cricket ground.

Salmon's Map of 1861 shows how far the progress of building in the Meadows had gone and this was to continue until the end of the 19th century, partly because some of the land north of the river was in Wilford. The Borough Extension Act 1877 brought this part into the borough.

The development of the Meadows resulted in a district of mainly working-class houses together with shops, public houses, churches and chapels, schools and industry. The latter included factories and workshops, in many cases adjoining houses. The area was already served by the River Trent, Nottingham Canal and from 1836 by the Midland Railway, all of which helped industry. Another incursion was the building of the Great Central Railway, which crossed the Meadows by bridges and embankments. The building of Arkwright Street, Wilford Road and the improvement of London Road completed the connection to the town.

One hundred years after the Enclosure Act many of the houses were unfit for habitation as laid down by the provisions of Housing Acts. They were in the main too small and overcrowded to be capable of improvement. The clearance of these started in the 1960s and the opportunity was taken to also get rid of non-conforming industry. A new plan for the redevelopment of the area was primarily designed to separate through traffic from the residences. This was achieved by closing most of Arkwright Street and Wilford Road with new traffic routes on the perimeter. The type of housing, too, was radically different from the old, with flats and maisonettes arranged in small groups instead of in terraces and streets. Some of the later 19th-century development remains largely unchanged.

The Meadows
One of T.W. Hammond's drawings of the Meadows before the Enclosure Awards. This one shows the famed crocuses. Mrs Annie Gilbert, who died in 1866, wrote a poem *The Last Dying Speech of the Crocuses*, the last line of which read 'Dread Spirit of Inclosure come — thy wretched will be done!'

Salmon's Map of 1861
This map showed the development which had taken place by 1861. This section shows Queen's Walk down to the River Trent.

Whey House

This rural scene of the Meadows before the Enclosure Act was painted by R.A. Moore in about the 1850s. The Whey House was listed in *White's Directories* as being on the east side of Queen's Walk somewhere between Kirkewhite Street and the Meadows. It ceased to be included when the Great Central Railway line was built.

The Porter's Rest, Cromford Street

This public house appears in a directory dated 1864, as a beerhouse occupied by Job Camm. He was still the occupier in the 1881 directory at 4 Cromford Street with the name of The Porter's Rest. It was thus named no doubt because of its nearness to the Midland Station. It was even nearer to Arkwright Street Station, which was built at a later date. The large building next door with a hoist was said to be at one time the Bread and Flour Society Mill.

The Rifleman Inn
This public house is shown in the 1881 directory as being at 17 Kirkewhite Street East, near London Road. It was still there in the 1956 directory.

Trent Bridge in 1815
This engraving is reproduced from John Blackner's *History of Nottingham*. It shows the north bank and some of the narrow arches of the bridge. The large building on the left with three chimneys was the waterworks. Water was pumped from the River Trent up to a reservoir on Park Row.

Trent Bridge about 1870
This view of the many-arched bridge was taken from the south bank downstream.

Trent Bridges 1870
After the new Trent Bridge was opened in 1869 the old bridge was retained for a time. The photograph shows how the new bridge met the old one in the north near the Town Arms.

London Road

This photograph and the next one would appear to have been taken from the upper floor of the Town Arms. Most of the buildings on the south side were demolished for the erection of Turney's leather works in 1911.

Arkwright Street

This photograph was taken before the tram track was laid down. The vacant site in the centre was later developed with a chapel, houses and the Globe Cinema. The excavation on the left was from the demolition of the waterworks.

Queen's Walk

This photograph is said to be of the west side of Queen's Drive taken in the 1920s. It is probably earlier than that, when it was still called Queen's Walk. There were 60 large houses in 1881 between Kirkewhite Street and the end of Wilford Road. The Cremorne public house was the building at that point.

Queen's Walk

This reproduction of a picture postcard was probably printed between 1900 and 1910. The houses on the left look to be the same or similar ones to those in the previous picture.

Arkwright Street

This photograph was taken after the railway bridge leading to the Great Central Railway line was built. The shop on the right, No. 65a, first appears in the directory for 1913, being a butcher's shop of Thomas Bernard Whitby.

Newthorpe Street

This picture was taken in September 1916 to show damage caused by a German Zeppelin air raid. This raid had caused damage to other properties near the Midland Station. The Mayor of Nottingham wrote to the Home Secretary saying that this had happened because the railway company had not screened the lighting, thus helping the airship to locate targets.

L. Cripwell

St Gabriel's Church

This church on Bathley Street was erected in about 1905 as a mission church. It had been paid for by Henry Abel Smith to try to encourage working-class people to attend who might be put off attending St Saviour's Church, which was only a few 100 yards away. Built of corrugated iron, it was probably intended to be less intimidating than a more formal church. It later became a daughter church to St Saviour's but has since been rebuilt in brick and used by another denomination.

L. Cripwell

Mundella School

In the 1890s the Nottingham School Board erected two new large schools to provide education beyond the elementary standard. Both became secondary schools in 1905 after the City Council had taken over the School Board's functions. One of these was the Mundella School in the Meadows. It was named after A.J. Mundella, a former MP for Nottingham who had been a government minister for education. The building was demolished in the 1990s.

Nottingham City Council

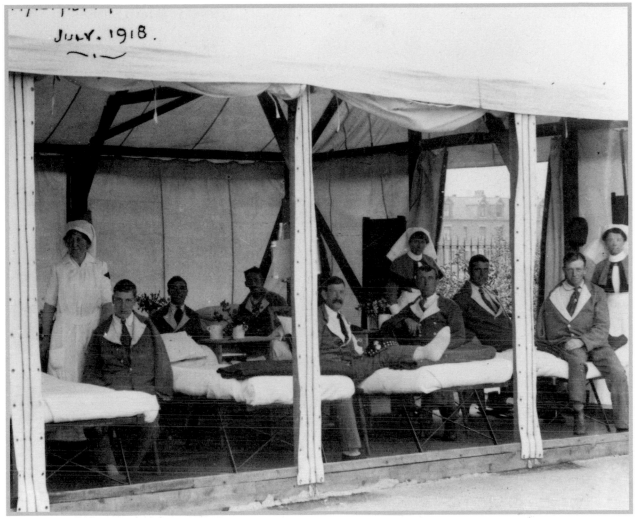

JULY. 1918.

Wartime hospital, 1918

During World War One many thousands of troops received injuries which required treatment. Many of them were transferred to Britain and were treated in temporary hospitals. One of these is shown in the picture above, which is thought to have been in the Trent Bridge School for girls in Green Street.

Victoria Embankment

In 1900 the City Council showed commendable foresight in creating the mile-long roadway from Trent Bridge to Wilford on the north bank of the River Trent and forming steps down to the river.

The picture postcard shows the Trent Bridge end with gates which could be closed, as the road was not a public highway.

Kirkby Street
After properties on Arkwright Street had been demolished, the rear of commercial buildings on Kirkby Street became visible.

Kirkewhite Street
This section of Kirkewhite Street in the centre of the picture revealed how much demolition had been carried out by the end of 1974. The building on the left was the British Rail office. It is still there and is used as a community centre.

The entrance to the city
The junction of Arkwright Street and London Road was pictured in about 1914 with a tram, the decorative lamp standard
and the Globe Cinema.

Railway Bridge
The LNER line crossed the Meadows on embankments. When the line was closed the bridges over streets were demolished
on Sundays.

Arkwright Street and Queens Road
The increase in commercial activity in the Meadows led to the Nottingham and District Bank erecting a new branch in 1894.

Burton's Almshouses
The Almshouses at the corner of Ryehill Street and London Road were built in 1859 with money from a Miss Ann Burton.
They were demolished under the 1970s clearance scheme and new ones erected with another charity near St George's Church.

London Road

This view of London Road looking north was taken from near Burton's Almshouses before clearance started. Most of the buildings, mainly large houses, were demolished as far as the former Arkwright School.

Bertram Street

This was a small cul-de-sac off Crocus Street. The entrance was through a tunnel and the houses went right up to the rear of factories.

Curtis Terrace
This view of the rear of houses was taken in 1974 and indicates how necessary the clearance campaign was.

London Road
This shows how after the houses on London Road were demolished, an earth bank with trees was created to reduce the traffic noise from London Road.

THE LACE MARKET

The area bounded by Fletcher Gate, Carlton Street, Goose Gate, Belward Street and High Pavement has been known as the Lace Market since the late 1840s. This site was the original Anglo-Saxon borough which grew to be the heart of the English borough when the Normans created the French borough. The English part by the 16th century was largely undistinguishable from the French, but in the 18th century it became a fashionable district containing large houses with gardens and orchards. As Nottingham became more industrialised later in the century, many of the inhabitants moved out to pleasant rural surroundings. The large houses found a ready source of accommodation for hosiers, who could live in them and also use them as warehouses.

In the 19th century the hosiery organisation declined and the large houses lost their status. Lace had begun to outstrip the hosiery industry and lace manufacturers who used the large houses for their businesses. Many of them found that it was convenient for them to have their warehouses near to each other and this led to the term 'lace market' being applied to the area.

By this time the lace industry was becoming a steam-powered factory, one with the need for new purpose-built warehouses. The second half of the 19th century saw buildings of the large architecture designed warehouses by using up vacant sites used as gardens or orchards. At the same time smaller houses were built to house the growing number of workers in the warehouses.

The first half of the 20th century saw two changes which affected the Lace Market. The industry itself declined and underwent structural changes, leading to the former warehouses being used for other commercial purposes. At the same time, modern transport and the action of the building of houses elsewhere reduced the need for housing in the Lace Market. Many of the older houses, often in yards, alleys and courts, disappeared.

These processes were accentuated in the 1940s because of war and 1945 saw the Lace Market in a poor physical shape and with economic difficulties in the use of the former warehouses. Wholesale demolition was a possibility but awareness of the area's history resulted in the Lace Market area being declared a Conservation Area. A gradual transformation over the last 40 years, encouraged by the City Council and government with co-operation from industry and commerce, has now almost finished, creating a new Lace Market. The 21st century fittingly came in the form of the NET trams along Fletcher Gate to the city centre and beyond. The building of new dwellings and conversion of some of the warehouses has brought the Lace Market to a residential area once again.

Part of Adams' Building, Stoney Street

This photograph shows part of the Adams' Building on Stoney Street, which was unusual in an industrial building. It is the entrance and windows of a chapel, which was a part of Thomas Adams belief in bringing religion to his workers. They were encouraged to attend a 15-minute service in the chapel before starting work in the morning. Their pay included the time so spent. The front has since been well renovated.

Nottingham City Council

Old Town Hall, Weekday Cross

The centre of the government had for centuries been in Weekday Cross, administered from what was known as the Guild Hall. The building in the picture became known as the Old Town Hall, after a new Guildhall was built in 1888. The engraving dated 1808 differs slightly from Wigley's similar one of 1791. The Old Town Hall was demolished when the Great Central Railway was built.

St Mary's Church

The 15th-century perpendicular style church replaced one on the same site. It became the 'mother' church of the town. The photograph shows the church from St Mary's Gate and is dated *c.*1890. The distant buildings on Stoney Street were demolished to form a site for lace warehouses.

High Pavement

This photograph is dated 1873. It is of an old building which pre-dated most of the other buildings in the area. It was probably demolished shortly afterwards as there is no mention of Hutten and Price in directories.

High Pavement

The photograph was taken in 1944 when the buildings adjoining the Shire Hall were being used as an annex to house various departments of the County Council. When most of the staff were moved to County Hall in West Bridgford, the buildings were used by magistrates sitting in courts in the Shire Hall.

Nottingham City Council

High Pavement Chapel

Until 1982 the building on the south side of High Pavement next to Garner's Hill was a Unitarian Chapel, the building erected in 1876 replacing earlier ones. High Pavement and Castle Gate chapels were the first nonconformist chapels to be built in Nottingham following the passing of the Toleration Act of 1678. The High Pavement building is now a restaurant, 'The Piano and Pitcher', and the Unitarian Chapel is on Plumptre Street. The photograph of 1873 shows the entrance to the chapel yard.

56 High Pavement

A Grade II listed building, 56 High Pavement is the last building on the south side of the street. The facade shown in the photograph, dated about 1903, does not match the elegant rear with a Venetian window. The rear view was only revealed when the building next to it was demolished after air raid damage in 1941. It was for many years St Mary's vicarage until another residence on Standard Hill replaced it. Fifty-six High Pavement then became used by commercial concerns and later as the County Council's Public Assistance Department.

Nottingham City Council

Stoney Street

The building in the centre of the picture, with the town arms, was the Free Grammar School until the new boys' high school was erected on Forest Road. It was then used for various purposes, including the wartime WRVS. It was demolished in 1961.

Stoney Street

This was the main through route from the south until Arkwright Street was built. It was developed in the 19th century with lace warehouses, most of which are still there but used for other purposes. The photograph was taken in 1964. Barker Gate is on the right.

Pilcher Gate

The street connects St Mary's Gate with Fletcher Gate. The name was given as the home of glove makers. All the buildings on the left-hand side have been demolished except the one on the corner of Halifax Place, which has been modernised.

Halifax Place

This building was looking the worse for wear in 1940 when the photograph was taken. It was formerly a chapel. It has since been renovated and houses the Lace Market Theatre.

Broadway

This short street only 200 feet long was laid down in the 1850s to connect St Mary's Gate with Stoney Street. The new warehouses on either side were for Richard Birkin's new warehouses designed by T.C. Hine. Birkin had acquired Plumptre House, adjoining St Mary's Church, and had demolished it for the site. The other section of Broadway, from St Mary's Gate, has a curve, which almost hides the above view.

Commerce Place

This small terrace of houses was on the north side of Barker Gate. The railings at the end of the yard separated the houses from a burial yard. The government ordered the burial yard to be closed as it was too near the houses. The photograph was taken in 1919.

Mrs J. Spencer

Barker Gate

These properties photographed in 1946 were on the north side of Barker Gate, which sloped down towards Lower Parliament Street. On the left of the photograph is a length of water pipe, put there for fire fighting.

Barker Gate

These two properties were 35 and 35A Barker Gate. J. Pinder's on the right of the photograph can be seen in part of the previous photograph. Both were listed in *Kelly's Directory* for 1956, the last one published. They were demolished to make way for Belward Street.

Daykins Yard
Situated between 57 and 59 Barker Gate at the eastern end, the yard formed part of the area which was cleared of property in the 1930s to build a new road from Parliament Street to Canal Street.

Wool Alley
This photograph is described as the site of the former Catholic Apostolic Church in Wool Alley, off Woolpack Lane, and as having been taken in the 1860s. The church was a group of Christians under apostolic rule who believed in an imminent second coming. In 1881 the church was in Northumberland Street.

Nottingham City Council

Cherry Place

Situated on the south side of Woolpack Lane, Cherry Place had back-to-back houses in 1910. The City Council had just appointed a Housing Committee and Cherry Place was one of the first to be condemned and demolished.

Rose and Crown public house

The licence for this house was refused in 1921. It was at the junction of Count Street and Newark Lane, both of which disappeared when the new Lower Parliament Street was made. In 1910 there were 350 public houses in the city, of which 14 were in the Lace Market.

Nottingham City Council

Nottingham City Council

Bellar Gate

Bellar Gate stretched from Hollowstone, the house on the left being on that street, to Barker Gate. The photograph was taken in 1944, when the streets still had cobblestones. The large building on the right was the rear of the Ice Stadium.

Nottingham City Council

Hollowstone

This drawing of Hollowstone was by Thomas Hammond, done in 1902. He was able to make some of Nottingham's streets appear much more attractive than they were. Hollowstone was the main entrance into the town from London Road before Arkwright Street was made. It was formerly steep and had to be reduced when heavy traffic had difficulty in ascending.

Plumptre Square

The shops with large advertisements were between Narrow Marsh and Malin Hill. The Town Arms on the right was at the bottom of Malin Hill. It was damaged by fire about 20 years ago, and remained derelict until recently when the area was redeveloped.

Commerce Square

Starting on High Pavement opposite to the south transept of St Mary's Church, Commerce Square widens and then leads to Malin Hill, a short steep footpath as far as Short Stairs. The picture is dated about 1890 and a directory of the period listed 138 milliners and 11 straw bonnet makers in the area.

Hollowstone

Taken in 1964, the view from the end of Dean Street shows the Roman Catholic Church of St Patrick, which was demolished and the name transferred to a new building in the Meadows.

Short Stairs

This steep flight of steps connects Malin Hill with Short Hill. The painted sign is on the rear wall of the public house. The photograph was taken in 1940.

Fletcher Gate
The Windmill public house was at the corner of Pilcher Gate and Fletcher Gate. When it was demolished, the site was used as an outdoor refreshment area. The whole area was regenerated in the large-scale redevelopment a few years ago.

Weekday Cross
The west side of Weekday Cross extended as far as Byard Lane. The Crown and Cushion public house also offered entertainment in the Palace of Varieties in 1910.

ARBORETUM TO ALFRETON ROAD

The area between what is now the Arboretum and Alfreton Road had for centuries been known as the Sandfield, from its geological structure. It had been one of the common fields and until 1845 it was not available for building. This was because the burgesses had rights which were then bought out by an Act of Parliament, the General Enclosure Act. The act appointed commissioners to administer the laws of the act by allocating the land to owners and it also ensured that some parts of the land were to become open public spaces. For the Sandfield area this was to become the Arboretum.

The planning procedure took many years because of legal and procedural matters and the first new buildings were not built until about 1860. There had been a pleasant country walk from the town along which the two main thoroughfares were to be Shakespeare Street and Waverley Street. There was already some access to the area as the General Cemetery had been laid out under a private act.

The section to the east of Waverley Street was planned for larger houses intended for the manufacturers and professional classes. Were street names such as Shakespeare, Dryden and Addison calculated to attract the better educated? On the west side of Waverley Street, the area was developed in two quite different ways. From Cromwell Street to Forest Road, the residential style of the east side continued, with the poetic cachet of Burns and Tennyson. A new church, All Saints, gave its name to this part.

Towards Alfreton Road working-class houses with terraces were built to house the workers of the large factories, some used as tenement style for lace or hosiery where small manufacturers could rent space.

The 20th-century combination of change in industry and smaller families without servants saw the gradual decline of the larger houses into multi-occupation and deterioration of houses. After World War Two the whole area was designated as a cultural, educational and administrative centre. This has only been achieved on the education side, with the gradual growth of what eventually became Nottingham Trent University. Some rebuilding of older houses has taken place on the east side, while the west side has seen the establishment of the Raleigh Village. This includes new modern housing replacing the older ones and some of the industrial premises converted to flats.

The Arboretum

The Enclosure Act of 1845 ensured that open spaces were to be left in various places. One of these was 12 acres from Sherwood Street (later increased to 17 acres). The council noted that 'the diversified nature of the ground and the saleability of the situation recommend this spot'. Samuel Curtis, who had designed Victoria Park, London, was appointed to carry out the work at a cost of £1,018, of which the two entrance lodges cost £580.

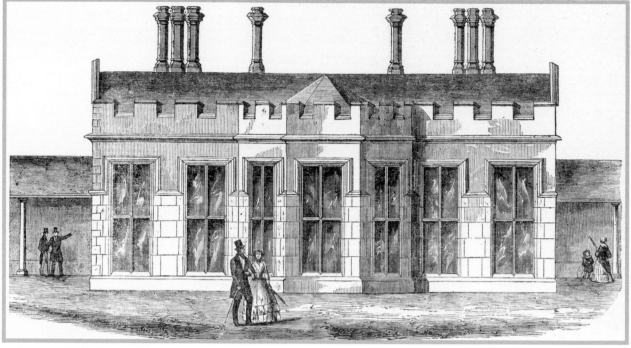

Arboretum Refreshment Rooms

In June 1851 the council approved the provision of refreshment rooms with a residence at a cost of £1,500. Smoking was prohibited both in the rooms and the grounds. The engraving does not show the wide wings which were added later. The rooms were adapted some years ago as a public house, although this had been damaged by fire recently and has since been demolished.

Arboretum, Addison Street

The eastern entrance to the Arboretum is on North Sherwood Street, with a tree-lined walkway which goes under a bridge on Addison Street. The photograph, taken about 1895, shows that the scene is still largely unchanged. The Arboretum was officially opened on 11 May 1852 when a crowd estimated at 25,000 attended.

Statue of Fergus O'Connor

In February 1859 the council agreed permission for a statue of Fergus O'Connor to be erected in the Arboretum. He had been a leader of the Chartest movement which campaigned for electoral reform. A petition against this protested that there was nothing in his public character or principles to recommend it. He had also been elected as an MP for Nottingham.

General Cemetery

This was a proprietary cemetery of the Nottingham General Cemetery Company under a private act of 1836. The main entrance is at Canning Circus, through an archway between houses erected by the freemen in compensation for their loss of grazing and other rights. It sloped down to another entrance on Waverley Street. With most town churchyards being full by that time, the General Cemetery was used extensively until it too became full. The City Council took it and maintains it as a footpath because of the historic importance. The photograph is of one of two chapels, both of which have now been demolished.

Nottingham City Council

L. Cripwell

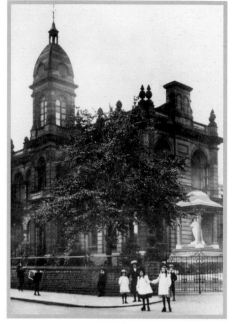

The School of Art

Replacing the Government School of Design on Heathcoat Street, the school was erected on Waverley Street in 1865 by the Town Council. Its original function was primarily to teach students to design patterns for the textile trades. It later widened its scope with courses for sculptors and artists, the latter including Dame Laura Knight and her husband Harold. Its name was changed to the College of Art and is now part of Nottingham Trent University.

Bonington Statue

Richard Parkes Bonington (1802–1828) was born at Arnold but lived most of his life in France. He painted many French scenes. His statue with a canopy designed by architect Watson Fothergill stood in the grounds of the College of Art on Waverley Street. It was later moved to storage at the Castle Museum but has been re-erected in Arnold.

Nottingham City Council

Nottingham City Council

Peel Street

When the former Sandfield was developed under the Enclosure Act, it was specifically designed for larger stylish houses for the wealthier middle class. Peel Street ran from Waverley Street in a west to east direction to Mansfield Road. It was laid down in 1852 but complaints were made in 1866 that it was not complete. Southfield House was the first house on the north side, next to the School of Art. It was demolished to form part of the site of the Women's Hospital, now converted to flats.

Dryden Street

This photograph dated about 1900 was of Dryden Street looking north from its junction with Shakespeare Street. The odd numbers 1 to 27 and even numbers 2 to 36 were also known as the Esplanades. This section of the street was redeveloped for new buildings for what is now Nottingham Trent University.

A.P. Knighton

George L. Roberts

Bilbie Street

This short street from Goldsmith Street to Shakespeare Street had only 14 houses, all on the west side. The east side was Horsefair Close, later the site of University College. The houses were demolished in 1963 and their sites and the street itself were used for an extension to Trent Polytechnic.

Addison Street

One of the first new streets to be laid out in the 1860s, Addison Street started at Forest Road and sloped down to Peel Street. Addison Villas, shown in the photograph, were on the east side even numbers 2 to 22 between Annesley Grove and Peel Street.

Nottingham City Council

Nottingham City Council

Mansfield Grove

The date of this photograph is not really known but must have been before 1881, as the houses are all shown in the directory of that year. It was a short street, with only eight houses on the right-hand side. The two houses at the side of the steps were on Peel Street. All these houses have now been demolished.

North of Shakespeare Street

Most of the older properties between North Sherwood Street and Waverley Street have been demolished. Some parts have been developed with new houses, but a major part has been used for the expansion of Nottingham Trent University. This view from Gill Street was taken after the houses had been demolished.

Gamble Street

This photograph of industrial buildings at the junction of Gamble Street and Newdigate Street shows how close industrial concerns were to the houses on Gamble Street.

Alfreton Road

The east side of Alfreton Road was within the borough while the west side was in Radford. Nos 2 to 168 in 1881, as far as Forest Road West, contained five public houses as well as small shops with living accommodation. They included all the usual food shops, as well as craftsmen such as boot and shoemakers, braziers, tinnex brush and basket makers. There were also two essential finance houses – pawnbrokers – there were 30 in the town listed in the directory. The shops in this photograph have been demolished and new modern buildings erected.

Raleigh Street
The former Raleigh Street Infants School occupied the vacant site awaiting development. The large factory on the left is on Russell Street and the houses at the top are on Tennyson Street.

Raleigh Street
Another view of the cleared site looking eastwards shows houses on Walter Street.

Gamble Street

The houses were on the east side of Gamble Street and opposite the former Lendal Square. The one on the left has a style more ornate than the others. The differences in the styles reflect the fact that most houses of that period were built in small numbers often by different builders.

Gamble Street and Thoroton Street
The photograph shows how industrial buildings and factory chimneys were close to houses in this area.

AROUND NORTH SHERWOOD STREET

Until William Dearden's map of 1844 was published, earlier ones did not show any part of the borough northwards beyond what is today Shakespeare Street. Dearden's map showed a narrow strip of buildings on Mansfield Road west side and on the east side of North Sherwood Street. These stretched from opposite what is now Woodborough Road as far as the Jews Cemetery, which had been built in 1823. To the west of North Sherwood Street the Sandfield had not been enclosed.

Jackson's map, which was based on surveys between 1851 and 1861, revealed that both sides of North Sherwood Street with streets leading off it was almost fully developed. *Wright's Directory* of 1881 listed 170 buildings on the street itself and terraces leading off it. There were five public houses, three of which had names which still survive. There were also shops, two tenement factories and various crafts such as plumbers, boot makers, painters and joiners.

After World War Two, many of the smaller working-class houses here and elsewhere were almost 100 years old and often with only basic necessities. Most of those on North Sherwood Street, as well as industrial concerns, were demolished in order to implement the planned redevelopment as a civic centre. This did not materialise as envisaged but did provide sites for new housing offices and light industries.

North Sherwood Street
This photograph, taken in 1972, shows the junction of Shakespeare Street and North Sherwood Street. The YWCA building on the left was opened in 1936 but is now a hostel for Nottingham Trent University. The public house on the right was then the Clinton Arms but has had name changes since. On the left-hand side of North Sherwood Street a car park has replaced the buildings which have been demolished.

North Sherwood Street

The car park in the previous picture continued to be used until it became the site of the new building for the Mechanics Institute to replace the other one in Burton Street. The building at the rear is the Jewish Synagogue in a former Methodist Church.

Duke of St Albans public house

The smallest public house in Nottingham was demolished shortly after the date this photograph was taken in 1963. It was at the corner of St Albans Terrace on the east side of North Sherwood Street.

George L. Roberts

114

Reg Baker

North Sherwood Street

The Hole in the Wall in the picture dated 1973 was at the junction of Huskinson Street. The public house is still there but all the other buildings have been demolished and Huskinson Street has been built on with other new houses.

Nottingham City Council

Bluecoat Street

This scene photographed in 1970 has a vastly different appearance now. Taken from the eastern end of Bluecoat Street at the junction with Mansfield Road, it shows the end of Woodborough Road. On the right is the wall at the north end of what was Victoria Station. The York Street bus station and a car park have been built above the site of the station. The building at the junction of Huntingdon Street was formerly occupied by East Midlands Gas Board but has since been demolished, with flats erected on the site.

Balmoral Road

This short road connects Forest Road with Arboretum Street. The building was the first secondary school for girls to be used by Nottinghamshire County Council. It was named Brincliffe School in about 1890. It had previously been Tudor House School and it is now part of Nottingham Girls High School.

North Sherwood Street

This building, No. 67, was known as Cutts factory. It was occupied by nine users. The photograph was taken in 1963.

The Bluecoat School

The photograph, taken about 1920, shows the Bluecoat School from Mansfield Road. It moved to the above premises in 1853 from High Pavement. It was moved again to Aspley Lane in 1967.

Nottingham Boys High School

This was former Free Grammar School founded in 1513 by the will of Dame Agnes Mellors, the widow of a mayor. The building in the picture shows the new building erected in 1868 when it was given its present name. It has entrances on Waverley Street and Forest Road. It is one of the leading public schools.

117

Mansfield Road and Forest Road East
This picture, dated about 1900, shows the end of Forest Road East and, on the right, the main entrance to the Church Cemetery. It was opened in 1856 and has many interesting tombstones. The decorative lodge has been demolished.

North Sherwood Street
This small group of houses was known as Bourne's Place. The windows on the top floor were designed to give maximum light for working on stocking frames.

Bluecoat Street
The building on the left, demolished in about 1900, was latterly known just as the New Church. When it was founded it was called the New Jerusalem Church (Swedenborgian).

North Sherwood Street
This view of a comparatively new industrial building shows the Bluecoat Street flank at the junction of North Sherwood Street. It has been demolished and replaced by a block of flats.

Former Bluecoat School
One of the doorways of the former Bluecoat School has a replica of the town arms and a statue of a boy dressed in the old school uniform. Both these were formerly on the original school building on High Pavement.

Forest Road East
This photograph would have been taken in the 1900s and apart from the tram lines it does not look very different today except for the ladies' attire.

MAPPERLEY

Thomas Maperley was described as a man of distinction during the reign of Richard the Second who acquired some land to which his name was attached, later altered to Mapperley. These lands were, in fact, in Basford parish, which extended as far as what is now Woodborough Road. However, the name Mapperley Hills became attached to the land to the north east of Woodborough Road. When Basford parish became part of the borough in 1877, the name seems to have been applied to both sides of Woodborough Road.

Under the Basford Enclosure Act of 1792, the Wright family was awarded land which later became Mapperley Park. Ichabod Wright built a mansion, Mapperley House, which was the only house shown on Sanderson's map of 1835. This showed a number of brick kilns in the area.

When the borough's Enclosure Act of 1845 started to develop the former Clayfield, houses were built on both sides of Woodborough Road. This former track soon became a major road with streets leading off it, as far as Mapperley Road. From there the road was called Mapperley Hills Road but later was changed so that Woodborough Road formed a continuous road as far as the borough boundary. A small private estate of large houses was built called Alexandra Park and some of the roads leading off Woodborough Road were given names such as Hamburgh Road and Mecklenburgh Road, although in World War One these were altered to English names because of anti-German feeling.

From the 1880s onwards the land between Mansfield Road and Woodborough Road was gradually developed with larger houses as a rival to Nottingham Park. Much of the building did not take place until the Edwardian era. The east side of Woodborough Road continued to be developed up to 1900 with streets running off it and parallel to it, such as Blyth Street. This area is still largely unchanged.

A large development took place on the borough boundary, Porchester Road. This was the building of a large psychiatric hospital, at first known as the Borough Lunatic Asylum but later changed to Mapperley Hospital. It was set in extensive grounds reaching as far as the Wells Road.

Alexandra Park

This picture, taken from the end of Mapperley Road, shows the entrance to the park on Woodborough Road in 1910. Alexandra Park was a small residential estate developed in the 1850s. The first house on the left through the gates was Fernleigh, then occupied by one of John Player's two sons, John Dane Player. The house was acquired in 1949 by Nottingham City Council as an elderly persons' home, now it is Nottinghamshire Hospice. The building on the right was a garage and the land to the right of it was used for the building of Alexandra Court.

'Springfield'

This large house in Alexandra Park, Springfield, was the home of Sir John Turney in 1900 and later of A.W. Black, one time MP. Later it became the National Children's Home and Orphanage.

Malvern House

This large house with extensive conservatories is on Mapperley Road. In 1879 it appears in a directory as the home of Thomas Butler Cutts, a lace manufacturer. At one time in the 1950s it was occupied as offices by the National Coal Board but is now a doctor's surgery.

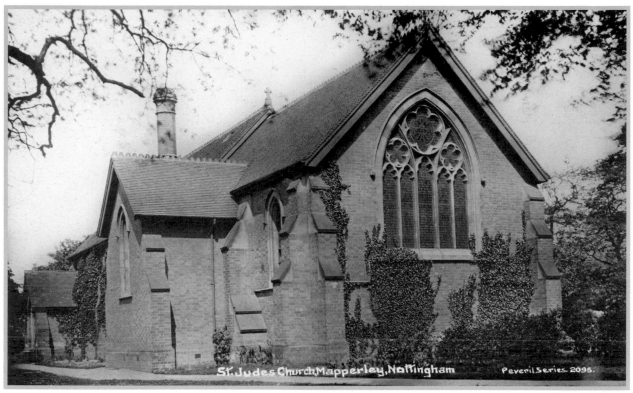

St Jude's Church

Situated on Woodborough Road, near the junction with Lucknow Drive, the church was built over a long period, from 1877 to 1925. Its earliest services were held in the offices of the Mapperley Brick Company.

Redcliffe Road

This road existed as Red Road before building commenced. The date of the photograph is stated to be between 1910 and 1920, but is probably much older as there are 21 houses listed in a directory of 1902.

Magdala Road

Some of the earliest houses in Mapperley Park were built in Magdala Road. Although the house in this photograph is not mentioned, it appears from the gate posts and road to be one of them, probably No. 5. Magdala was a fortress in Ethiopia which British forces stormed in 1868 to free an imprisoned British Consul.

Children's Hospital

The hospital was founded as a charity in 1869 in Postern Street. In 1900 it moved to the above building, on Chestnut Grove, off Mapperley Road, given by Thomas Birkin. When the new hospital, Queen's Medical Centre, was opened in 1978, some smaller hospitals, including the children's, were closed and the patients transferred to the new hospital.

'Cowley' Victoria Crescent

Victoria Crescent is on the south side of Private Road, which runs from Mansfield Road to Woodborough Road. For most of its length a through route for traffic is restricted to residents who have a key to a barrier. In 1910 it was occupied by Professor Ernest Weekley of the University College, as it then was. He became well known as the writer of books on philology, the study of words and language.

Mapperley Brick Works

This aerial view of about 1930 shows Woodborough Road on the right, running from bottom to top. In the centre, with an industrial building, is Morley Avenue. Later in the 1930s council houses were built on the rest of the site. The brickworks at the top of the photograph produced a large number of bricks in the 19th century and up to the 1950s.

Nottingham City Council

Mapperley Plains

This view was taken in about 1900 from the end of Woodborough Road. The continuation, known as Plains Road, had Arnold on the left and Carlton on the right. The houses on the left of the photograph are still there on Woodthorpe Drive, formerly Scout Lane.

Nottingham Historical Film Unit

Mapperley Tram Terminus

The growth of housing along Woodborough Road, Plains Road and adjacent areas made it viable to provide a tram service. By 1910 there was a service from Nottingham to Mapperley with a tram every six minutes.

Mapperley Hospital

Nottingham had a general psychiatric hospital from 1812. An Act of 1853 made local authorities responsible for mentally-ill people, overseen by a Lunatic Commission. Nottingham Corporation had Mapperley Lunatic Asylum in 1880 on high ground overlooking the town on Porchester Road. The change in the name reflected the growing recognition of the need for treatment in place of incarceration. Responsibility was transferred in 1948 to the National Health Service. The buildings in the photograph were nurses' homes.

No. 10, Querneby Road

From the junction of Ransom Road and Woodborough Road, Querneby Road was laid out parallel to Woodborough Road in the 1870s when Mapperley was expanding. The name appears to commemorate a Nottingham family called Quarnby, one of whom became mayor of Nottingham in the 17th century, although the name was more generally given as Quernby. The properties shown in the photograph of 1983 were demolished as part of a site used for new offices.

Reg Baker

Mapperley Brickworks
A view in 1955 taken from Woodthorpe Drive. The land in the foreground had been quarried for clay and is now occupied by new housing.

Woodthorpe Park
Woodthorpe Grange and its land were purchased by the City Council and laid out as a public park in 1921. Running through the park then was part of the Nottingham Suburban Railway. It passed under Woodborough Road through a cutting with a station at Sherwood. It then passed through a tunnel and a bridge under Woodthorpe Drive to Daybrook.

ST ANN'S

The Clayfield was the other large common field which was made available for development under the Enclosure Act 1845. It was on the east side of the borough and extended northwards as far as the Basford border and eastwards to the Sneinton and Carlton ones. In the north east, gardens had existed for some time on the sloping Hungerhills.

The enclosure award provided, as elsewhere, some open space, in this case a walk extending from Mansfield Road to Cranmer Street and another one, Robin Hood Chase, from Woodborough Road to St Ann's Well Road.

The size of the area meant that most of the houses were for the working classes and for industry nearby. The area was divided into two halves by a new main road, St Ann's Well Road. A west to east area from Mapperley Road area to Carlton Road was named Alfred Street, with three sections – north, central and south. From Mansfield Road a track northwards went to villages such as Lambley and Woodborough, and was renamed Woodborough Road.

Jackson's and Salmon's maps both set out in detail the parts which were built up by 1861. The area to the south west of the Alfred Streets were virtually complete. St Ann's Wells Road has progressed even further for about three quarters of a mile. Progress in building continued throughout the 19th century – the building of new churches gives a guide to the pace of development. St Marks, Windsor Street, was erected in 1856, St Lukes, Carlton Road, and St Ann's, St Ann's Well Road, both in 1863, followed by St Matthias, Carlton Road 1869, Emmanuel, Woodborough Road 1885 and St Catherines, St Ann's Well Road 1896 and St Bartholomews, also 1896. Only two of these remain, neither of which are used as churches.

Its size meant that probably the majority of the occupants were of what were known as the 'lower orders' – unskilled labourers and similar jobs, which in those days relied on muscle power and were low paid. However, St Ann's was by no means a one-class suburb. Robin Hood's Chase, as it was known in 1902 in a directory, listed 140 houses. The occupations included several teachers, clerks, a pianoforte tuner, a bookbinder, a watch repairer, a journalist and a factory manager. Samuel Ward was a yeast importer who later became a mayor of Nottingham and James Shipman, FGS, both lived there. The latter was the author of articles and books on archaeological excavations.

As elsewhere in Nottingham, the post-1945 years saw a gradual ageing of the houses built up to a 100-years earlier. In St Ann's many of them were too small and lacking modern facilities to be improved. When the slum clearance commenced in 1954, St Ann's was not one of the first to be dealt with. In 1967 the City Council approved Phase I of clearance, which was followed by six further phases up to 1970. Unlike some earlier clearance schemes, which left some industrial areas out, St Ann's was a more comprehensive redevelopment. This was designed to eliminate much of the through traffic routes, thus enabling the residential areas to be built on garden city lines and without multi-storey flats.

Berkeley Street
This was one of a number of streets which ran parallel to St Ann's Well Road on the south side. The photograph was taken in 1967 shortly before the 21 houses were demolished. They were built as model dwellings in 1852–54 by a group headed by William Felkin, mayor of Nottingham in 1850 and 1851.

Working Mans Retreat

This building on Plantaganet Street is still there, having escaped the widespread demolition of properties in the clearance areas. The sign tells that it was built in 1852, mainly through the generosity of George Gill. Occupiers had to show that they had some female relation who could look after them if becoming incapable. If they had no such relation they had to have a weekly income of up to 10 shillings a week to pay for such help.

Nottingham Evening Post

Ashley Street

A small street of nine houses and a sheet metal works. Ashley Street connected Manchester Street with Alfred Street South. The photograph, taken in 1939, shows workmen building a street air-raid shelter. It would also be used as a warden post.

George L. Roberts

Handel Street

Handel Street and the adjoining streets are shown on Salmon's map of 1861 but are not mentioned in a directory dated 1853. The photograph taken in 1959 from near Carlton Road is looking westwards towards Victoria Baths. The initials on the flank of the building on the right-hand side are of G.A. Wheatcroft (see the next entry).

George L. Roberts

Handel Street

This picture, also taken in 1959, was of the junction of Handel Street and Liverpool Street. Twenty-three Handel Street was the home and probably workplace of George A. Wheatcroft, the last entry in directories being in 1916. The house is said to be the birthplace of Harry Wheatcroft, the well-known rose grower.

Nottingham City Council

Bath Inn

Built in the 1860s at the corner of Handel Street and Robin Hood Street, the Bath Inn had a decorative door frame. This public house has now been refurbished and presents a very different picture to the one above.

Reg Baker

Salford Street

Taken shortly before demolition in 1972, the photograph shows the Gospel Hall at the junction of Salford Street and Liverpool Street. It was described as a Gospel Hall in directories in the 1950s but on earlier maps it is called a boys' school.

George L. Roberts

Edwin Street

Taken in 1964 from Bombay Street, this photograph shows the short Edwin Street, which went from St Ann's Well Road to Hungerhill Road. The building on the right was St Ann's Well Road School. All the properties were demolished in the redevelopment.

Blue Bell Inn

No. 90 Robin Hood Street was the Blue Bell public house. It was at the junction of Alfred Street South. Built in the 1870s, it appears to be vacant awaiting demolition in 1972 when the photograph was taken.

Nottingham City Council

George L. Roberts

St Bartholomew's Church

Built in 1896 on Blue Bell Hill Road opposite Sketchley Street, St Bartholomew's Church became a separate parish in 1905. As the land sloped steeply down to St Ann's Well Road, the church became a prominent landmark. It was demolished in 1971.

St Ann's Well Road

No. 123 St Ann's Well Road was a branch of the National Westminster Bank in 1972 when this photograph was taken. It stood at the corner of Alfred Street Central. It had been built in about 1899 as a branch of Nottingham and Nottinghamshire Banking Company, which later became Westminster Bank.

Corporation Road
This view is looking eastwards towards Blue Bell Hill Road, where St Bartholomew's Church can be seen centre left. It shows how comprehensive demolition had been.

Stretton Street
This was a small street off Union Road, which backed on to a newly-built warehouse erected on the site of St Marks School. The houses present are completely different styles.

Alfred Street/Gordon Road

For a short time this small site was almost rural looking. It had formerly been occupied by a small estate, Stewart Place, which had been built to a prize-winning design in a competition for working-class dwellings.

Huntingdon Street

On the edge of the worn-out housing of St Ann's, the advertisement reflects a different world in 1966.

CITY CENTRE

The term 'City Centre' is something of a misnomer, as it is only two miles from its southern boundary but six miles from its northern one. This is, to some extent, the result of the boundary extensions, which took place between 1877 and 1952. From early mediaeval times it had been the geographic centre of the borough after the Anglo-Saxon borough and the French borough became integrated. As each had its own market places, until then it was natural for the open space to be retained not only as a market place but also as an economic and administrative centre. As an important regional centre it became known as the Great Market Place. Here the twice-weekly markets were held, for the sale of everything in the years before shops became part of the economy. Its annual Goose Fair became widely known until it was moved away in the 1920s.

It attracted favourable comment from travellers who visited it and wrote about it. Celia Fiennes, who visited Nottingham in 1697, described the largest market place in England in glowing terms. 'Out of it', she wrote 'ran two very large streets much like Holborn, but the buildings finer, and there is a piazza all along one side.' One side had stone pillars for walks, which still survive today.

In 1728 a new building was built at the east end of the square, called the Exchange, which was used for the council's business as well as for commercial purposes. It was there until 1926, when it was demolished and the present Council House was erected on the site. At the same time the market itself was transferred to a new indoor building on King Edward Street. Goose Fair was moved to Nottingham Forest and the cleared site used to form a processional way, steps, gardens, fountains and underground toilets.

The site has now been completely redesigned and opened this year. Traffic has been removed from Long Row, the steps removed to form a flat surface with an ornamented pool. New toilets have also been provided nearby.

Long Row, with three sections – east, central and west – formed the north side from Clumber Street to Chapel Bar. The other streets around the Exchange were Smithy Row, Cheapside and Poultry, while on the south side was South Parade, formerly known as Timber Hill.

Until 1864 the only traffic route north of the market square was Sheep Lane, which was widened and renamed Market Street. There were a number of pedestrian routes to Parliament Street, two or three of which still remain. The rest were all closed and the crowded insanitary houses on them demolished and two new streets built in 1895, King Street and Queen Street. Other thoroughfares, which gave access to the south and west, were Mount Street, St James Street, Friar Lane, Wheeler Gate and Exchange Walk.

The late 19th century saw the increased amount of traffic entering the square. Horse-drawn and later electric trams, omnibuses and motorcars all helped to make the Market Square the hub of the centre of Nottingham. Trams and trolley buses disappeared but omnibuses and motor traffic increased, causing congestion. Various alterations such as one-way streets and pedestrianisation eventually meant that the area around the Old Market Square, as it had been known since the 1920s, was restricted mainly to public transport. The new tram, *Nottingham Express Transit*, comes down Market Street and along South Parade and Cheapside to complete the transformation and the new council square.

Badder and Peat's Map 1748
This map shows how much of the area around the Old Market Square had been developed by the middle of the 18th century.

Nottingham City Council

The Old Market Place
This engraving is dated about 1820 and shows its spaciousness when the market was not being held. The building at the far end of the Exchange was built in 1728.

Old Market Square
This is one of the few photographs taken showing Chapel Bar, Angel Row and St Barnabas Cathedral. It was taken in the 1880s.

Old Market Square

This photograph was taken on the 17 November 1928 and shows the last time the market stalls were held. The Council House was still under construction with scaffolding around the dome.

Old Market Square

This photograph was taken a year after the previous one with the layout and the dome completed. This view was, apart from minor changes, to remain unaltered for the next 80 years.

Nottingham City Council

Spencer Higson & Co

George L. Roberts

Old Market Square
This photograph was taken in 1949 on the occasion of the visit of Princess Elizabeth and the Duke of Edinburgh. It shows the ceremonial role whereby royal visitors passed along the walk to the Council House with a guard of honour.

Old Market Square
In 1997 the Queen visited Nottingham to celebrate the centenary of the Royal Charter granting Nottingham the status of city and walked along the traditional ceremonial way.

Old Market Square
A last look at the square before the bulldozers moved in.

Exchange Arcade
This sketch done in about 1930 shows one of the three entrances to the arcade with its shops and offices above them. This one is on the south side, with Cheapside facing The Poultry.

W.L. Eveleigh

Long Row

This photograph, dated about 1860, shows the main section of Long Row East. It was separated from Long Row West by the narrow Sheep Lane. This was widened in 1865 to become Market Street. The building on the left was the Talbot Inn (see next picture). The bottom of the picture is described as a furniture market.

The Talbot Inn

This is a painting by Thomas Cooper Moore, an artist who painted many Nottinghamshire scenes. The inn was mentioned in a directory of 1832 but was probably much older. The figure on the roof was of a talbot dog, a hunting hound. The inn was demolished in 1875. Yate's Wine Lodge now occupies the site.

Long Row

Dated about 1900, this photograph shows how much Long Row had become a shopping centre. Most of the buildings remained as shown for the next 50 years.

Long Row

This picture taken in 1971 from South Parade when buses ran along Long Row. The upper storeys of the shops have remained largely unchanged. The one on the corner of Queen Street was designed by Watson Fothergill.

Long Row East
The Black Boy Hotel was built in the 1870s to a design by Watson Fothergill. The statue in the centre of the picture was of Samuel Brunt, an 18th-century benefactor whose charity owned the site. The hotel was demolished in the 1960s despite public protests.

Long Row East
As Walter Ball's plumbing business was in Maypole Yard, a board at the entrance on Long Row was needed to help find it. The entrance disappeared when Skinner and Rook's shop was demolished.

Cheapside

Cheapside ran from the rear of the Exchange to High Street. The photograph, taken in 1926, shows George Harris's billiards rooms and Thraves furniture store.

Poultry

Opposite Cheapside this photograph taken in about 1905 shows the Flying Horse Hotel. It was demolished about 10 years ago and a shopping arcade built on the site. This connects Poultry with St Peters Gate. The arcade is named Flying Horse Walk.

145

Exchange Walk

This pedestrian way connects South Parade and Poultry with St Peters Gate. It was probably widened in the 1880s from a narrow alleyway. A directory for 1881 lists 14 shops. The photograph, dated 1938, is interesting as it shows how fashionable outerwear was compared with that in pre-1914 photographs, as well as with todays.

Smithy Row

Smithy Row was on the north side of the old Exchange. One of a number of shops occupied the site until the Exchange was demolished. The one in the picture, a jewellers, was at the corner of High Street.

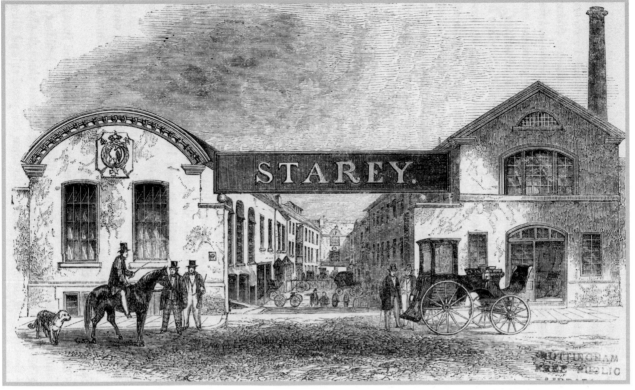

Lincoln Street

This engraving appeared in a guide to the Great Northern Railway of about 1857. The 'carriage manufactory' was on Lincoln Street between Clumber Street and Clinton Street. *White's Directory* for 1864 gives Thomas Rawston Starey as the occupant, describing him as Captain Robin Hood Rifle Corps, his residence being Daybrook House. He was a borough councillor from 1865 to 1874 and a biography about him can be found in Robert Mellors's *Men of Nottingham and Notts.* (1924).

Lincoln Street

The standpoint of this 1936 photograph may well have been the same as that for Starey's Coach Manufactory. It is from Thurland Street looking north. The high wall extended along both sides of Clinton Street and Parliament Street. It was to protect a few yards of the LNER railway track, which was not covered. Trains from Victoria Station came underneath a tunnel below Parliament Street before entering another tunnel under Thurland Street to Weekday Cross. When the Victoria Centre was built shops were erected over the site, perhaps with basements.

Clumber Street

This photograph is dated about 1895 and is of the west side of Clumber Street. The shop in the centre is that of Hindley's music shop, hence the sign 'Pianos, Organs, Violins'. Arthur Hindley was the occupant in directories from 1893 and the business was still there in 1965 under the same name. Hindley's was No. 21, while next door at No. 29 was Baldock and Company, drapers. The reason for this is that Nos 23, 25 and 27 were at the rear, approached through a passage. No. 23 was a veterinary surgeon's, W.E. Taylor. The figure of a horse can be seen in the photograph to advertise this.

Maypole Yard

This yard was off Clumber Street, between Nos 29 and 31. The photograph is dated about 1900 and directories show No. 31 as empty about that time and it seems to be in a poor state. It was probably used on a temporary basis for the exhibition advertised as 'Life in Paris'.

Pelham Street

This house is described as having been the home of Mrs Francis Byron, great aunt to Lord Byron. This would no doubt have been in the late 18th century. The photograph is said to be dated 1850 but this seems unlikely to be correct as it is so early. The house is opposite the Durham Ox Inn, which was on the north side.

16 Clinton Street East

The earliest mention of this shop being a locksmiths in directories is 1950. As it was a limited company it may have been in existence under another name and elsewhere. Until a few years ago when it closed it had been synonymous with the name 'locksmith' to most Nottingham people.

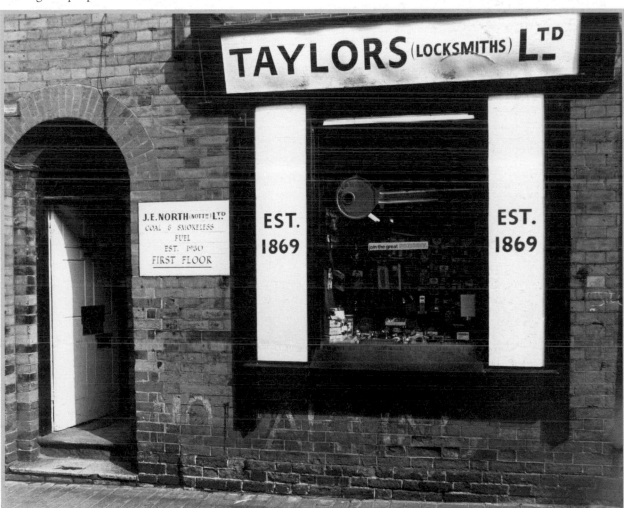

Bottle Lane

This photograph was taken in 1971 from Fletcher Gate showing Bottle Lane, a narrow street which sloped down to Bridlesmith Gate. The building on the left had originally been built as a chapel in 1819 but had been used for commercial purposes for many years. After it was demolished about 12 years ago, the site was used for car parking. Work commenced on building The Pod in 2005, a hotel, restaurant and retail scheme. The Queen Elizabeth public house on the left of Bottle Lane was demolished in 2006.

Bridlesmith Gate

The Dog and Bear public house is no longer in the premises shown, which are now retail shops, but the decorative features remain. This one shows a dog and another one a bear.

SOUTH OF THE CITY CENTRE

The Anglo-Saxon settlement on the cliff above the marshland needed little more than footpaths running southwards through the Meadows to the River Trent. This was easily fordable near to where the first bridge was built. This was in AD920, at the insistence of the English king, being partly to enable the better defence of the borough, but also as a means of communication between the north and south of the country, particularly important as it was a halfway stop between London and York. This meant creating a more formal road, later known as the Flood Road, now London Road. This led via Hollowstone to Stoney Street for access to the north.

The occupation of a Norman borough and the building of the castle eventually led to the construction of streets running east connecting the two boroughs. Castle Gate from the Norman borough met the Pavements – Low, Middle and High. When the Norman church of St Peter was built, Hounds Gate joined the two boroughs with St Peter's Gate.

The Normans had altered the course of the River Leen to provide water for the castle and this formed a natural barrier with bridges over the River Leen. Wheeler Gate and Lister Gate led out of the square and Greyfrier Gate continued, leading to a footpath to Wilford through the Meadows.

The second half of the 18th century saw a tripling of the population of the borough, which led to the building of thousands of small houses in any available land south of the centre. This resulted in the creation of a district, which was to become one of the worst insanitary areas of the town. This was not helped by it being on marshy undrained land, unlike the higher ground on sandy soil with natural drainage.

In 1794 the Nottingham Canal was built and replaced the River Leen to some extent. It brought increased trade to Nottingham. The main route south from the city centre was not direct from Wheeler Gate to Lister Gate but had to traverse a small street from St Peter's Church to Low Pavement. An improvement in the early 19th century was the building of Albert Street to form a direct link. The coming of the first railway in 1834 with a station on the south bank of the canal led to the building of an extension to Lister Gate. Named Carrington Street with a bridge over the canal, this led eventually to the opening up of Arkwright Street through the Meadows.

Had anyone suggested in the 1860s that all this would be reversed in a 100 years time they would have been laughed at. Yet it happened. It started with the clearance of the Meadows and the closing of Arkwright Street as a through route. The building of the Broad Marsh Centre caused half of Carrington Street to disappear and the pedestrianising of Albert Street and Lister Gate completed the story. Wheeler Gate has survived with at least some traffic in one direction only.

Wheeler Gate
In 1962 Wheeler Gate was the first part of the route from the Old Market Square to Trent Bridge. Building of a tall block on Friar Lane was in progress after properties at the corner with Wheeler Gate had been demolished.

J. Buist

St Peter's Church
This photograph was taken in 1898 from a point at the end of Hounds Gate. The space in front of the church seems to be a horse-drawn cab rank.

Albert Street
This shows a royal visit by the Queen when the Royal Show was held at Wollaton Park in 1955. The photograph was taken from the churchyard.

Albert Street

Albert Street was constructed in 1846 to connect Wheeler Gate direct to Lister Gate, instead of the inconvenient way via Church Gate. The photograph was taken about 1900, so the tram would have been a horse-drawn one.

Lister Gate

The name is of great antiquity and comes from the term 'litsters', meaning dyers. The date of the photograph is 1928. Most of the buildings have since been rebuilt, although No. 29 on the right is largely unchanged.

T.W. Wyncoll

Broad Marsh

This photograph is dated 1893 and most of the buildings were later replaced. Some of them did survive until the 1960s when the Broad Marsh Centre was built. The shop at No. 29 Lister Gate, seen in the previous picture, still has a Broad Marsh street sign on its wall.

Walter Fountain

This structure stood at the junction of Lister Gate, Carrington Street and Greyfriar Gate. It was demolished in the 1950s. John Walter, to whom it was dedicated, was MP for Nottingham in 1842 and later became the editor of *The Times* newspaper.

F. Walden Stevenson

Carrington Street

These almshouses on the west side of Carrington Street were Collin's Almshouses, built in 1830 to supplement another block on Friar Lane. Both were financed by members of the Collin family, who were descendants of Laurence Collin, master gunner at the castle in the civil war. Other members of the family married into the Smith family. One of them, Robert, was made Lord Carrington, after whom the street was named.

The small building on the left was a police box from where policemen could ring headquarters.

Carrington Street

The photograph, which is undated, refers to the Thomas Smith Obelisk. He died in 1727 and had been Abel Collins executor, so would no doubt have been a member of the banking family. The obelisk was in the grounds of the Collin's Almshouses, opposite the bottom end of Stanford Street. The building on the right was occupied by H. Pooley and Sons, weighing machine makers. The photograph must have been taken before 1932, as Pooley's were not there then. The obelisk probably was demolished much earlier.

Nottingham City Council

Carrington Street

This photograph shows the buildings, mainly shops, on the east side of Carrington Street, from Broad Marsh to Canal Street, in about 1920. W.E. Jackson trunk manufacturers were at No. 61.

71 Carrington Street

This appears to be a handbill or advertisement in a newspaper. In a directory of 1879 William Carver was described as grocer and tea dealer at 71 Carrington Street, with his home at 89 Queens Walk. Francis Carver, no doubt William's son, appears as the occupier until 1895 when E.S. Poyser, jewellers, took the shop over. It was at the junction with Canal Street on the north side.

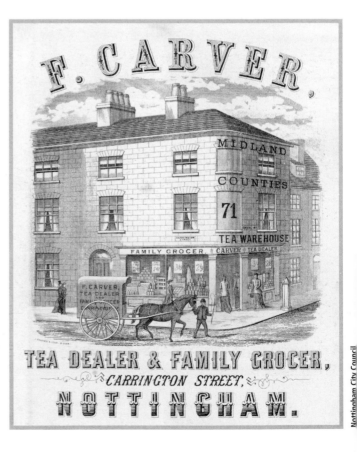

Nottingham City Council

Carrington Street

The shops on Carrington Street look newer than those in the photograph on page 156. This photograph is dated 1934 and the shops and the Lincoln Arms public house did not alter in appearance when they were demolished to make way for the new bus station in the 1960s.

Nottingham City Council

Carrington Street Bridge

Until the 1840s, Carrington Street ended at the Nottingham Canal. Once the railway station was opened on the opposite bank of the canal, the Corporation were under pressure from the railway company to build a bridge over the canal. It was completed in 1842. The drawing was done by Thomas Hammond in 1901.

Nottingham City Council

Level Crossing

Nottingham's first railway station was on the west side of Carrington Street. When a new line to Lincoln was opened, a second station was opened near the London Road end of Station Street. This meant that some trains had to cross Carrington Street through a level crossing. It took many years of negotiation to remove this source of delay to traffic. Pedestrians complained that the gates closed so quickly that they could be trapped between them. The crossing can just be made out on the photograph dated 1860, looking north from the end of Queens Road.

Midland Station

The only railway station still in use in the city was built for the Midland Railway in 1904 and has not changed in its external appearance, apart from the tram lines, in this picture of 1905.

Nottingham City Council

SOUTH WEST OF THE CITY CENTRE

The two main streets westwards from Wheeler Gate and Albert Street were part of the French borough, but both had been converted into fashionable residential streets by the 18th century. The 19th century saw industrial and commercial replacement of the houses, Castle Gate seeing less of this than Hounds Gate. The 20th century completed the process by the construction of Maid Marian Way, which bisected both streets.

Before Carrington Street was made, Lister Gate continued via Greyfriar Gate to the canal and River Leen bridge with a footpath through the Meadows to Wilford. By the 1840s the area bounded by Castle Gate, Greyfriar Gate, Canal Street and Castle Road became an overcrowded working-class housing area with a number of new streets. Greyfriar Gate developed into a relatively good shopping street.

By 1930 slum clearance had transformed most of the area east of Carrington Street and the City Council made a Finkhill Street clearance area which saw the demolition of about 300 houses, some of them back to back with closed courts – little different from the areas which the Health of Towns Commission in the 1840s described. Some of the photographs in this chapter show the appalling conditions that were still present. Some of the children shown in them, if they survived, will still be alive today in their 70s and 80s.

Economic conditions in the 1930s were such that nothing could be done to regenerate this area once the houses had been redeveloped. The outbreak of war in 1939 prolonged the process until the 1950s, when the Peoples' College was built and Maid Marian Way was started. Even then there was a delay until it could be finished beyond Hounds Gate.

Angel Row

The short stretch of street from St James Street to Mount Street was opposite Long Row. The name is at least 500 years old and is probably from angelus bell, from a nearby mediaeval religious house. The photograph is dated about 1900 and the name Barker on the flank of the building was the name of a cabinetmaker, and later it became a shop of Henry Barker, Smart and Brown. It is now Nottingham Central Library.

St James Street

Taken in 1944, this photograph shows the south side of St James Street, which started at the junction of Beastmarket Hill. No. 11 was occupied by J. Hughes wholesale stationers and No. 9 was also a wholesale merchants. This building was rather neglected until a few years ago, when it was well restored to its former Georgian town-house status and is a well-appointed restaurant.

Spaniel Row

From Friar Lane to Hounds Gate, Spaniel Row only had buildings on the east side after Collin's Almshouses were erected on the west side. In *White's Directory* of 1902, No. 1 was a hard confectioner's, No. 2 a picture framer and No. 3 an insurance and house agent. Next door was an Apostolic Church (see also page 97).

Castle Gate

The two houses on the north side of Castle Gate were adjacent to Newdigate House. The picture is said to be dated 1890 and the houses, with their Flemish-style gables, were probably early 18th century. They were demolished when Maid Marian Way was built.

Castle Gate

This view shows the rears of Castle Gate properties on the south view near Castle Road. The land behind the gate marked 'Marsh and Creassey Yarns' was used as the site for the office of the department of Social Security.

The Salutation Inn

'Ye Olde' has been dropped from the name shown on the wall of the building in the photograph of 1952. Since Hounds Gate bisected Maid Marian Way, the main entrance is now on that road, although not as picturesque as the Hounds Gate view. The public house vies with the Bell Inn and the Trip to Jerusalem as one of the three oldest Nottingham inns. The Salutation has interesting cellar caves.

Castle Gate

This photograph taken in 1922 shows the end of St Nicholas Street, which connected Hounds Gate with Castle Gate. The house at the junction on the right-hand side was demolished to widen St Nicholas Street. It was No. 50 and in 1920 it was a hairdresser's shop. No. 44 next door was also pulled down. Its two decorative pillars can be seen flanking the doorway in this photograph.

Nottingham City Council

Castle Gate

This photograph of the western end of Castle Gate was taken in 1950 before part of the street was used in making Maid Marian Way. St Nicholas' Rectory, which was demolished, can be seen as almost the last building on the right. The square-end house on the right does not have a flat roof, as can be seen from the Castle Grounds. Walnut Tree Lane on the right turned sharply and went as far as Chesterfield Street. Most of it became part of the site of a new People's College.

Castle Gate

This photograph shows the buildings to the left of the Royal Children public house before they were demolished to enable Maid Marian Way to be built.

Stanford Street

On the right of this picture taken in 1960 were the buildings at the southern end of Stanford Street, which were demolished later that year. Stanford Street runs downwards from Castle Gate but not a through street, stopping short of the Broad Marsh Centre. Newton's shop was at the corner of Stanford Street and Greyfriar Gate, the whole of which formed part of the site of Broad Marsh Centre.

St Nicholas Church

This picture dated 1955 shows the church from a viewpoint on the former Chesterfield Street after the houses were demolished in the 1930s. On the left of the church was a narrow St Nicholas Church Walk, at the end of which a flight of steps led down to Walnut Tree Lane.

Parr's Yard, Page Street

Page Street was a small street, 200 feet long, which ran parallel to Castle Road from the east end of Isabella Street. It is now buried underneath the Peoples' College. The photograph is dated about 1931 and would have been taken then as the City Council made a clearance order on the houses in that year. The houses on the left of the picture were in Parr's Yard, but they were back-to-back houses with others on Page Street. There was a tunnel entrance at the far end with houses on Mortimer Street above it.

Kenton's Square

This so-called square was on the north side of Edward Street, which was the next street up from Castle Road after Isabella Street to which it ran parallel as far as Page Street. The tall houses on the west side were not back-to-back as those opposite were, which were back-to-back with houses on Page Street. The 'square' had a house on Mortimer Street closing it but had a slight advantage over Parr's Yard, as the open end allowed the sun to be seen occasionally.

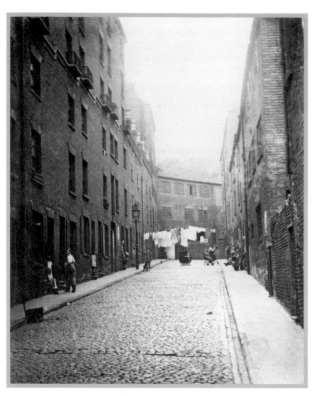

Castle Terrace

Castle Road rose steeply past Mortimer Street and just below Castle Gate to the right was Castle Terrace, with a public house, the Colonel Hutchinson, on the corner. The houses on both sides were tall, as was the row at the end of the street, which was on Mortimer Street. A view of the end houses of Castle Terrace can be seen way above those on Kenton Square.

Smoke's Yard

This charming scene of the north side of Mortimer Street no doubt deserved its name, but with coal fires everywhere else at the time it is difficult to see why it had the discrimination.

The Old Anchor Inn

Walnut Tree Lane ran from just below Castle Gate and carried down as far as Mortimer Street. An Anchor Inn on Walnut Tree Lane was listed in *White's Directory* of 1832. It was still listed as No. 20 in a 1956 directory but not as a public house. This was not surprising, as all the houses in this part of Nottingham had been demolished.

Castle Road

This view was taken from Finkhill Street when all the houses were still on it, as well as those on Edwin Street, Mortimer Street and one side of Isabella Street. On Castle Road there were buildings of the Corporation Water Department, The Trip to Jerusalem and Brewhouse Yard. The building opposite, on the right of the photograph, was formerly St Nicholas School and the buildings adjoining it were on Castle Terrace.

Nottingham City Council

Nottinghamshire County Council

Brewhouse Yard

This photograph of about 1900 shows that the first half of the 20th century saw a complete transformation. In the castle grounds there were still some of the buildings which had been built after the destruction of the castle in 1831. The Corporation Water Department's premises are still there but are now part of the Leisure Services Department. The houses to the left of the picture have been restored to become the Life of Nottingham Museums and the grounds landscaped.

Brewhouse Yard

Thomas Hammond's drawing of 1872 certainly shows a more attractive picture of Brewhouse Yard than the previous picture. Early maps of the 19th century show a long row of cottages in the open space. Brewhouse Yard was not within the borough until the 1860s and had an evil reputation as a refuge for debtors and others avoiding the long arm of the law.

Nottingham City Council

White Rents

This was an old almshouse, which stood at the south end of Greyfriar Gate. In 1884 the Town Council agreed it should be demolished 'on sanitary grounds alone'. It took another five years and a compulsory purchase order for the council to be informed that the site had been cleared and that a public vehicle weighbridge was to be erected on the site. This was demolished when Maid Marian Way was built.

George L. Roberts

Greyfriar Gate

This picture dated 1960 shows the junction of two streets on the west side of Greyfriar Gate – Chesterfield Street and Rosemary Lane. This consisted mainly of commercial buildings. Rosemary Lane was a narrow cul-de-sac at the rear of factories on Stanford Street while Chesterfield Street went as far as Walnut Tree Lane. Both disappeared under the Broad Marsh Centre.

Wilford Street
All the properties on the east side of Wilford Street were demolished when the redevelopment of the area between Nottingham Canal and the western end of Canal Street commenced. The cleared site on Wilford Street was used for the building of the *Evening Post* offices. The photograph dated 1996 showed the rear of the properties on Wilford Street and Canal Street.

Wilford Street

This view was taken in 1971 from the Wilford Street Bridge looking westwards along the canal. Most of the buildings on the north bank have been demolished and new flats and apartments erected.

Nottingham City Council

Woodward and Clark

This was the name of a firm listed in *White's Directory* of 1883 as Woodward, Clark and Company, timber and slate merchants, Castle Wharf, Castle Road and Wilford Street. The drawing is by T.C. Moore but it is not clear exactly where the buildings were, as Lenton Boulevard (later renamed Castle Boulevard) had not been built in 1883. The street layout may have been changed when the Boulevard was built.

SOUTH EAST FROM THE OLD MARKET SQUARE

From High Street another route led southwards as far as Low and Middle Pavement. Bridlesmith Gate is known by that name as early as 1304. It had been the site of the western defence of the Anglo-Saxon borough. At the beginning of the 20th century there were 48 shops, offices, public houses, a bank and a building society along it. In addition there were several sets of chambers, occupied by solicitors, architects, surveyors and the coroner's office.

Streets led off it to the Lace Market on the east side and the west side down to Albert Street. This commercial heart of the city and the Georgian splendours of Low and Middle Pavement gave way to a completely different Nottingham. Opposite the southern end of Bridlesmith Gate was the narrow steep Drury Hill, leading down to what had been marshes for centuries. For the previous two centuries it had grown into one of Nottingham's most unhealthy and notorious slums. Narrow Marsh as the area was generally known, and which confusingly was also the name of one of its principal streets, was a by-word for criminal activities as well. In 1902 in Narrow Marsh, the street alone had 10 public houses and also had a number of common lodging houses. These were mainly in tall houses backing on to the cliff and catered for vagrants, homeless men, women and children, herded into overcrowded rooms. The Borough Council tried to alter it by renaming it Red Lion Street but people refused to accept it. In 1905, however, the council officially altered the name to Red Lion Street.

The whole area between Carrington Street, Canal Street and London Road was in effect divided into two halves when the Great Central Railway from Victoria Station emerged from a tunnel at Weekday Cross and carried on over a viaduct. An attempt to deal with the improvement of the area was first proposed by a new Housing Committee of the council in 1910. This proved to be so radical a solution and expensive to carry out that it was not proceeded with. In 1923, thanks to government legislation and financial support, the council made a compulsory purchase order to acquire the unfit houses east of the railway line. This led to the wholesale clearance of the area and replacement of some of the houses by building new council houses on the former Red Lion Street and renaming it Cliff Road.

The area to the west of the railway had to wait a little longer before it could be cleared. The Sussex Street clearance order was made in 1931 but the cleared sites were not immediately redeveloped. They were used for a time as a 'bus station' until the 1960s, when the Broad Marsh Shopping Centre was built.

Pepper Street

Harley's Vaults was a wine and spirit merchants at the last property, No. 4, on the south side of Pepper Street. This short street is off the west side of Bridlesmith Gate. Until about 20 years ago, it crossed Church Gate at the bottom and continued past St Peter's Church to the square. When Marks and Spencer's acquired land adjoining the church the whole of Church Gate and part of Pepper Street became the site of an extension of its store. The top half of Pepper Street is still there.

Bridlesmith Gate

This photograph of 21 and 21A Bridlesmith Gate was taken in about 1925. One was a confectioner's and the other an antique furniture dealers, William Lee. The inscription on the adjoining building was part of the words 'General Garibaldi public house', which was demolished in about 1934 when the Gate Inn was built on the site. The others were not pulled down until 1945.

Bridlesmith Gate

Taken in the 1960s, this view was from Low Pavement looking north. Bridlesmith Gate was then a traffic route but as the 'no entry' sign shows, only from Victoria Street southwards. This was before it was pedestrianised.

Willoughby House

This house on Low Pavement was named after the Honourable Rothwell Willoughby, a member of the family which owned Wollaton Hall. It was built about 1738 and the engraving is from Deering's 1753 history of Nottingham. Its elegance has remained untouched and is now occupied by Nottingham-born Sir Paul Smith, the fashion designer.

Postern Chambers

This office block was on the south side of Middle Pavement. The section between Drury Hill and Middle Hill also had Severn's restaurant and a post office. All disappeared to form part of the Broad Marsh Centre. Severn's was saved and rebuilt but the handsome doorway of Postern Chambers did not survive.

Drury Hill

Opposite the southern end of Bridlesmith Gate was the narrow steep hill which led to Broad Marsh. In spite of strong opposition at a public inquiry, it was demolished as part of the site of the Broad Marsh Centre.

Broad Marsh

This photograph is said to be dated about 1890. The building was on Broad Marsh and the street sign on its flank is of Drury Hill.

Newbridge Street

At the rear of Carrington Street, this thoroughfare connected Canal Street with Broad Marsh. When this photograph was taken in about 1920 there were only 14 buildings on the two sides, mainly because seven side streets led off Carrington Street. Most of the buildings were demolished in the 1930s Sussex Street Clearance area or later to form part of the Broad Marsh Centre site. The Primitive Methodist Chapel facing Broad Marsh was destroyed by fire in 1949 when it was used for an exhibition celebrating Nottingham's Quincentary, having received its full status by a charter of 1449.

Leen Side

Until the Nottingham Canal was constructed the River Leen flowed from the west along a route which later became part of Castle Boulevard and Canal Street and into London Road and beyond. On its northern bank was the street which was appropriately known as Leen Side. It started more or less where today's tram crosses Canal Street. By the 1930s, as it was in fact the continuation of Canal Street, the name Leen Side was discontinued. The photograph was taken in 1909. Fleet Place and the whole of houses between Leen Side and Narrow Marsh were demolished in the 1920s.

F. Walden Stevenson

Red Lion Street

In 1923 the City Council made a clearance area and compulsory purchase order known as the Red Lion Street Scheme. All the houses and some other properties were demolished and a new street, Cliff Road, replaced Red Lion Street.

F. Walden Stevenson

Crossland Place

This photograph was taken in 1923 shortly before the City Council made the Red Lion Street clearance order. Crossland Place was a cul-de-sac, from Leen Side towards Red Lion Street. St Mary's Church can be seen in the background. The tall houses on the left had the windows on the top storeys dating from earlier times when they were designed to let in light for the framework knitters.

Kirk's Yard

The timber-framed building was known as the Old Farmhouse. Badder and Peat's map of 1743 depicted the area which became Leen Side later as comprising mainly gardens and fields, so it is possible the farmhouse was still in use then. It is doubtful whether it was still in use in 1919 when the photograph was taken. The background was the east end of High Pavement and Short Hill

Nottingham City Council

Red Lion Street

This photograph was taken after the whole length of Red Lion Street had been cleared of houses and other buildings. The viewpoint was from the site of the Old Farmhouse, about 1929. Malin Hill, which still exists, is the steep footpath running from left to right in the centre of the picture. Some of the rock face below it can still be seen today. The rear of 56 High Pavement can be seen on the left.

Nottingham City Council

Old Bakehouse

This photograph is dated 16 May 1931 and is a close-up of the remains of the building shown on the bottom left of the previous picture. It shows how buildings were built right up to the rock face with some rooms excavated in the rock.

Popham Street

This street, as it still does, ran from Red Lion Street to Canal Street. In 1913 when this photograph was taken, a directory listed several commercial firms, including J. and J. Vice Limited, printers and Fitchett and Wollacott, wood and stone turners. Both were still there in *Kelly's Directory* of 1956 and J. and J. Vice were still there in the only other post-1956 directory in 1968.

Popham Street in this picture has buildings on both sides of the street and the view also shows the spire of the then High Pavement, Unitarian Chapel. All the houses were demolished under the Sussex Street clearance order of 1931.

St John the Baptist Church

This church was erected in 1844 and just under a 100 years later it was damaged so badly in the 1941 air raid that it had to be demolished. It was on a site just off Canal Street near to what is now Shortwood Close, as can be seen in the photograph. It had been designed by a notable architect, George (later Sir George) Gilbert Scott, the architect of St Pancras Station and Hotel.

Nottingham City Council

Malt Mill Lane

This view of Malt Mill Lane looking south was taken from just beyond the railway bridge, which crossed it, as the Ordnance Survey shows that the street narrowed as shown in the picture. It ran from Red Lion Street to Canal Street. The date is said to be 1934, but it must have been earlier as there is no mention of it in a 1932 directory, nor is there a Fergus O'Connor in the list of public houses. It still exists today in a truncated form alongside the tram viaduct.

Nottingham City Council

Sussex Street

This photograph, taken in 1914, shows Sussex Buildings on Sussex Street. In 1831 it was called Turn Calf Alley. As Sussex Street it ran from Canal Street as far as Middle Marsh and Broad Marsh. Sussex Buildings must have been on the west side of the street, as on the east side were the end houses of the several streets named after the former orchards – Peach, Pear, Plum and Currant. These were at right angles to Sussex Street. On the west side were Harrington Street and Rancliffe Street with buildings between them. It seems likely that Sussex Buildings had shops on the ground floor with houses on the upper floor.

Sussex Street

This view dated 1931 was taken from near Harrington Street on the left and Currant Street on the right. The whole of the houses were demolished from 1931 onwards under a clearance order, which extended westwards towards Carrington Street. The cleared sites were not built on and for many years were used as an uncovered bus station.

Trent Street

This street crossed the Nottingham Canal between Canal Street and Station Street. The street on the right-hand side of the picture was Parkinson Street, which was built over in the 1950s when Boots office buildings were extended.

Atkey's motor car business occupied the ground floor at the corner of the two streets while the lace firm Nottingham Manufacturing Company had the upper floors. For A.R. Atkey himself, see page 23.

Broad Marsh

The clearance areas around Sussex Street and Broad Marsh remained undeveloped until 1971, when work commenced on building Middle Hill and the Broad Marsh Centre. The signal box was on the former LNER line, crossed Canal Street, the canal, Station Street and London Road on bridges to Arkwright Street Station.

Canal Street

This building was on the south side of Canal Street. To the right is part of the railway viaduct, which crossed over Canal Street. This was part of the line which after leaving the Weekday Cross tunnel turned level and went via High Level Station on London Road and then crossed the River Trent to Radcliffe-on-Trent. The railway and viaduct, as well as the building, were demolished a few years ago when development along the Nottingham Canal took place.

East of the Market Place

Smith and Wild's map of 1820 shows that eastwards from Long Row was Pelham Street and from Cheapside was Chandler's Lane. These met at a junction which in earlier times had no doubt seemed to have been an open space called Swine Green. By 1863 Chandler's Lane had been replaced by a new street called Victoria Street. The Borough Council gave its name despite there already being a Victoria Street off Derby Road. This was then renamed College Street.

The 1820 map showed that Swine Green had been renamed Carlton Street. From there, there was a single thoroughfare although it had two parts, one being Goose Gate and the other Hockley. Beyond there, as far as the Clayfield and the border with Sneinton was a new suburb, which had grown up in the previous 30 years to house the ever-increasing population of the borough. To the north were Cross Lane and Millstone Lane, with a more or less separate block of streets and houses. To the south were similar enclaves limited in size because of the nearness of Sneinton. This centred on Carter Gate and between these two was the largest block, east of Coalpit Lane (now Cranbrook Street) and Plat Street, dignified in an 1831 map by an additional 't'. This later caused the area as a whole to be referred to as Meadow Platts, although cattle would have found little to graze on.

The unreformed pre-1835 council was aware as early as 1829 that houses were being built in a way that caused concern. In that year it resolved that any Corporation lands leased for housing should be required to have outside walls at least 9" thick and that no back-to-back houses would be allowed. In each case, however, the Corporation could, in special circumstances, waive these conditions.

After the reform of the Municipal Corporation Act in 1835, the new council was occupied from time to time with conditions of working-class houses. Some limited measures involved demolition of unfit houses. Despite this, in the opening years of the 20th century doctors, clergy and others showed concern and were pressing for action. One letter to the council from a meeting of clergy claimed that the housing of the poor in some parts of the city were a disgrace to the community.

As a result the council, backed by new legislation, appointed a Housing Committee. Members of the committee visited the worst areas, of which the Meadow Platts was one, and embarked on a clearance of the Carter Gate area. This started just before 1914 and was only able to make limited progress because of the war. Work on such areas started up again after the war and the Meadow Platts area was also helped in the 1920s and 1930s by the extension of Lower Parliament Street through the area as far as Canal Street.

All this was reflected in the building of Huntingdon Street and its GPO sorting office, the construction of Sneinton Wholesale Market and the provision of new accommodation for the City Transport undertaking.

Carlton Street
No. 1 Carlton Street was the home and later the business of Wright's bankers, who eventually became part of Lloyds Bank. The building is now a restaurant.

Goose Gate

On the south side was the former Black Swan vaults. In 1960 it had closed and the sign shows what was about to happen to the premises. The premises have since been altered and are now occupied by a rather different kind of shop.

Colwick Street

This photograph is dated about 1910, which was before any of the houses in this area were demolished. Its length was practically co-terminous with today's Brook Street. However, the maps show that there were 17 streets all leading off Colwick Street and the picture may be of one of them, perhaps Washington Street. The picture does show that the streets in this area looked like, washing across them being the usual. The group of children on the right were perhaps listening to some entertainment.

Colwick Street

This photograph was taken in February 1934 and is identified as being Colwick Street before it became known as Brook Street. No. 29 was, as shown, at the corner of Bedford Row which still exists. On the left of the picture can be seen part of the men's hostel, Sneinton House, which had been built in 1929.

Colwick Street

This picture would have been taken about 1932, when *Kelly's Directory* listed the occupant of 17 Colwick Street as John Pownall, marine store dealer. Cavendish Street was about halfway along what is now Brook Street.

Colwick Street

This picture would have been taken in the early 1930s after the whole of the properties on the west side of Colwick Street had been demolished. The standpoint is said to be near Red Street, which is confirmed by Bath Street Schools on the top right-hand side.

Meynell Street

This was a short street just south of Beck Street. It was at the junction of Platt Street in the photograph taken on 15 April 1929. 'The Grapes' was a beer retailer, not a public house. It was demolished along with all the other property behind it to form part of the new road. The section of Platt Street as far as the new Parliament Street became Huntingdon Street. The large buildings on the right side of Platt Street were factories which remained.

Cross Street

This photograph was taken in May 1927 from a standpoint a few yards from that on page 187. In the centre is Meynell Street with 'The Grapes' beer retailer. Nile Row on the left was the next street along Cross Street and Nile Street was just beyond there. Cherry Street opposite went as far as Coalpit Lane, later called Cranbrook Street.

Brook Street and Cowan Street

It is easy to identify this scene as Brook Street extended to Beck Street, which is still there, and the tall building was the Britannia Arms, demolished a few years ago. The street at right angles to Brook Street is Cowan Street, which is still there from Bath Street. The photograph is dated 9 May 1913 and was taken after repairs had been carried out. The chalk marks on the corner house would have been made by the sanitary inspection for identification.

Fyne Street

This street ran parallel to the part of Brook Street shown in the previous picture as far as Beck Street. As it was dated 11 May 1914, the houses, Nos 28 to 46, would have been visited by a sanitary inspector.

Bromley Street

The street was between Brook Street and Fyne Street, with Denmark Street at its north end and Nile Street at its south end. The photograph was taken on 11 May 1914, another house with the date of inspection on the shutter. The two houses in the picture, taller than the others, must have been (at one time anyway) of better quality with shutters and a window box.

Platt Street

In the late 1920s the City Council decided to make a new street from King Edward Street to Canal Street/London Road. This was to reduce the amount of traffic going through the centre of the city. A short street, St John's Street, was widened and called Parliament Street. It then joined Platt Street from Beck Street and this section was renamed Huntingdon Street. The remainder of Platt Street was widened and renamed as the continuation of Parliament Street. It then went southwards superseding Sneinton Street and Carter Gate in a curve as far as the present-day traffic island at the end of Canal Street. The photograph was taken in 1930 showing work in the part facing north. There were streets running off Platt Street on both sides.

Nile Street

The photograph taken in 1934 shows the whole of this short street. It stretched between Lower Parliament Street to Brook Street and is one of the few streets which survived the clearance of this area. It is now at the south end of what was the GPO Sorting Office.

Fyne Street

This is another view of Fyne Street with houses on the east side to Beck Street and again the top of the former Britannia Arms can be seen. Denmark Street was about 40 yards from Beck Street. As the notice on the door indicates, the photograph was taken on 7 July 1914. The woman and children seem to have been asked to pose. Another human touch is the two window boxes on the first floor.

Washington Street

This was one of several streets, which ran from Colwick Street to Bath Street, that were cleared to form the site of the council houses on Brook Street.

Nottingham Historical film unit

Sneinton Market

The photograph is dated 1890s. The market is not actually in Sneinton, the boundary being about 20 yards south of the Albion public house. Salmon's map of 1861 shows an open space marked 'New Market'. It also shows Bath Street already in existence, as were the baths and wash houses, which were erected in 1850 under powers in the Baths and Wash Houses Act 1846. The building in the photograph was a later one on the same site, opened in 1896 and named Victoria Baths. Behind them is the tenement block Victoria Buildings.

Beck Street

This building was demolished about four years ago. It was the Britannia Arms, a distinctive building with each floor in a different style. The architect, Thomas Simpson, drew the plans for the building in 1875.

Huntingdon Street
This building was built in the 1930s as the General Post Office Sorting Department, on the cleared site of the district known as Meadow Platts. The northern rounded end occupies the land formerly used by narrow streets such as Meynell Street, Bromley Street and Fyne Street. It has now been increased in height, converted into a hotel and given the name Marco Island.

Barker Gate/Lower Parliament Street
This car park was in front of Nottingham Ice Stadium, the predecessor of the National Ice Centre. The site had formerly been a burial ground and when permission for it to be used as a car park was granted it was a condition that the trees were allowed to remain – they did, but not for long.

NORTH AND WEST OF THE MARKET PLACE

Between 1820 and 1861, four maps of the town of Nottingham were published. The first three, Smith and Wild's of 1820, Staveley and Woods's of 1831 and William Dearden's of 1844, were able to show the extent of the built-up part of the town. Each of them showed the south to north as starting at the canal and extending to Parliament Street and each covered the east to west extent from the border with Sneinton to the castle. All three showed that on the north side there was little or no building beyond Parliament Street because the common Sandfield had not been enclosed.

Smith and Wild's 1820 map showed that to the west building and streets existed as far as Park Row, the ancient limit and part of the site of the early town wall. The other two show the increased density of that area due to the increase in population from 1821 of 40,000 to 53,000 in 1841.

Jackson's map of 1861 covered a much greater area because of the new building, which had taken place under the Enclosure Act of 1845. His map extended to the Meadows in the south and to the whole borough to the north. The area beyond Parliament Street and as far as Shakespeare Street has been described in earlier chapters. The development up to the end of the 19th century included Holy Trinity Church, the Mechanics Institute, the Guildhall, University College, the Theatre Royal, the Empire and Victoria Station. In the 20th century Holy Trinity Church, Victoria Station and the *Evening Post* and adjoining buildings were demolished. The University College buildings after a number of educational changes became Nottingham Trent University. The shopping mall and flats were built on the former Victoria Station site and the end of the 20th century saw the end of all the properties between Trinity Square and Shakespeare Street.

On the west side the early Lammas Field enclosure saw the creation of a properly planned suburb of good quality houses, the St Barnabas Roman Catholic Cathedral, the Albert Hall and extensions to the General Hospital. The Ropewalk was built up early in the century before it became part of the borough. The area between Friar Lane and Park Row had become one of the most crowded working-class districts and it was not until the early 20th century that clearance took place. Full redevelopment did not take place until after World War Two with the construction of Maid Marian Way.

Mill Street

James Hargreaves was a Lancashire man who invented the spinning jenny for making cloth. His fellow workers resented this as they thought it would lose work for them. So in 1768 Hargreaves came to Nottingham and built a mill on a street off Wollaton Street. It was named Mill Street. Thomas Hammond drew this picture of the street in 1914.

F. Walden Stevenson

Bow Street

In 1923 F.W. Stevenson, one of Nottingham's best photographers, took this photograph of Hargreaves Mill on Mill Street, the name of which had been altered to Bow Street. He would no doubt have deliberately chosen the same spot to stand as Hammond. He would have decided to give a little more reality to the scene. The Mill was demolished in 1930 and the site of Hargreaves Mill was near what is today Poynton Street.

Empire

The Nottingham Empire Theatre of Varieties, to give it its proper title, opened for its first performance on 28 February 1898. It was on South Sherwood Street adjoining the Theatre Royal, which as the 1959 photograph shows had the two adjoining entrances. The music hall of the late 19th century tried to provide entertainment which was more respectable than the notorious 'free and easies'. The price of admission ranged from fourpence in the gallery ('the gods') to two shillings for a fauteuil. The music hall died when television came along and the Empire was demolished in 1969.

George L. Roberts

Theatre Square

This photograph was taken sometime in the 1920s, before the statue of Samuel Morley MP was removed. It had been intended to re-erect it elsewhere but an accident in transit destroyed it. It is surprising to see how spacious the square was then compared to today.

Burton Street

This is a watercolour sketch of the Cattle Market, which was formed on Burton Street where it remained until 1885 when it was moved to Eastcroft. This was because the site was required for the new Guildhall. The viewpoint was on South Sherwood Street looking towards Holy Trinity Church.

Nottingham Evening Post

Burton Street

This photograph was taken on 10 August 1957 from the junction of Burton Street and South Sherwood Street, looking west. Nos 10 to 36 on the north side were being demolished for the site to be used for buildings for Nottingham Technical College. The half-demolished building on the corner was the Greyhound public house. Part of the Masonic Hall on Goldsmith Street can be seen in the centre of the picture.

Milton Street

This photograph is said to be dated about 1895. Allowing for the occasional changes of numbers, No. 70 Allen and Wood, late Palmer, is listed as No. 68 in the 1895 directory with No. 70 on the left shown as Eastmans Limited, butchers, and Joseph Robinson, clothes dealer. The tunnel entrance led to Mechanics Square. All the properties on Milton Street and as far back as far as Newcastle Street were demolished for the Victoria Station.

J. Buist

Trinity Square

This scene is taken from Trinity Row in 1958, looking east to Milton Street and the Welbeck Hotel. Holy Trinity Church had been demolished and temporary shops were being built to rehouse tenants of shops on Trinity Row. The latter were demolished and new ones erected, with the former church site used for a multi-storey car park.

University College

Aided by an anonymous donation of £10,000, Nottingham Borough Council was a pioneer in establishing a municipal university college. The buildings shown in the photograph of 1900 are little changed today and when finished in 1881 contained the Free Library on South Sherwood Street and a Natural History Museum at the other end facing Bilbie Street. The college moved to new buildings at Lenton and became a university in 1948. The Shakespeare Street buildings are now part of Nottingham Trent University.

Hanley Street

This short street runs from Wollaton Street to Talbot Street. The building with the tower was part of W.J. and T. Lambert's bleachers factory. During reconstruction the tower fell but was rebuilt. The building to the right of Lamberts was demolished and on the right side of Hanley Street was the first electricity-generating station of the Corporation's undertaking. The street was named after Hanley Almshouses (see the next photograph).

Hanley Almshouses

The original almshouses were in Stoney Street but new ones erected in 1857 on Hanley Street. They were formed from a charity in the 17th century set up by a Henry Hanley or Handley. They were demolished in the 1960s along with the other houses, Nos 13 to 23 shown in the previous picture. The money from the sale of the site was used to erect new almshouses at Bilborough.

Chaucer Street

The white posts are at the end of Belgrave Square and the houses on the north side of Chaucer Street were demolished as part of the site for new buildings for Trent Polytechinic, now Nottingham Trent University. The photograph was taken in 1971.

George L. Roberts

Shakespeare Villas

This cul-de-sac on the north side of Shakespeare Street had 40 houses and other buildings at one time, on both sides of the street. Judging from the position of the taxi, the houses on the left were on the west side. The iron railings no doubt disappeared during 1939–45 for war weapons. The only buildings there now are those on the west side and are part of 50 Shakespeare Street, the Registrar's Office. The well-ventilated taxi was a Wolseley.

Nottingham Historical Film Unit

George L. Roberts

Clarendon Street

When this street was designated under the Enclosure Commissioner's Award it was called Cemetery Road, no doubt because it adjoined the General Cemetery. The owners of the houses built on it were hardly likely to favour such a name and it was changed to Clarendon Street. The section between Talbot Street and Chaucer Street had substantial well-built houses on both sides. Those in this photograph, taken in 1971, are Nos 2 to 30, and are mainly occupied as offices.

Nottingham City Council

Chapel Bar

This photograph was taken in about 1912 when the street was open to traffic from the Old Market Square to Derby Road. The street had been known by that name since the Bar, an entrance to the town, was demolished. The Bar had two rooms, one of which was a chapel for the guards, hence Chapel Bar. The shop on the right was a grocer's, Sale and Sons, while on the opposite side was W. Hickling's wine and spirits merchants. Chapel Bar was closed off when Maid Marian Way was made. Since all the buildings on the west side were demolished and new ones erected, the area was renamed Chapel Quarter.

Park Row

Taken in 1944, this photograph shows the junction of Chapel Bar and Park Row. Barclays Bank was No. 25 Chapel Bar. No. 1 Park Row was a post office and the two large windows on the first floor were from the old House of Commons when it was burnt down in 1834. They were saved when these properties were demolished for Maid Marian Way.

Park Row

Park Row Chambers, No. 11, and Nos 13 and 15, were on the south side of Park Row. On the left of the photograph, taken in 1944, was Park Place. They were mainly occupied by solicitors and similar professions. Like those in the previous picture, they were demolished as part of Maid Marian Way.

East Circus Street

The area beyond Park Row was the first development on land in the common lands under an Enclosure Act of 1839. Wellington Circus formed the centre from which other streets radiated, including East Circus Street. The photograph taken in 1960 shows the east side, which had five large houses either side of the classically-styled hall, which at one time was Nonconformist chapel. The next photograph shows what happened in 1971.

Park Row and East Circus Street

This photograph, dated 1971, was taken from Park Row looking north showing the junction with East Circus Street. The hall and the houses between it and Wellington Circus had been demolished and the Playhouse erected on the site. Behind it can be seen the Albert Hall and St Barnabas' Cathedral.

203

Mount Street

This street in 1958 ran from Chapel Bar to Postern Street, as it still does today. The only part still existing is the building on the south side, then under construction. On the left of the picture is the end of the row of buildings shown in the previous picture and in front was a temporary building. All were to disappear to make way for the northern half of Maid Marian Way.

Marriotts Square

This dilapidated house, photographed in 1912, had been visited by the sanitary inspector, hence the chalk marks on the door. Repairs were later carried out. The square was off Granby Street, which ran from Friar Lane to Park Row and is now mainly part of Maid Marian Way.

Granby Street

This photograph taken in 1958 was from Amberley Street, looking north east. The street, a short one, connected Postern Street with Cumberland Place. The long row of buildings in the centre of the picture were on Granby Street, on the south-east side. In front the use of the cleared site as a 'bus station' can be seen.

Rutland Street

The area between Friar Lane and Park Row had some of the worst houses in Central Nottingham in the 1920s and a clearance in the 1930s removed them by demolition, although little redevelopment took place before 1939. The City Council were seeking to have a new relief road on the west side to fulfil the similar one on the east side, via Lower Parliament Street. Rutland Street was one of the streets in this area, between Granby Street and Standard Hill. In 1913 when this photograph was taken, Booth Place was on the south side of Rutland Street. A truncated part of Rutland Street still exists off Standard Hill.

Standard Hill

This view of the former General Hospital was taken in 1959 before a new Trent Wing was built. It was demolished when the hospital was closed and new offices and apartments were built on the cleared sites. The main hospital building was retained and is used as offices.

Postern Street

This photograph was taken in 1971. Mount Street is on the left and Amberley Street on the right. Postern Street runs from left to right, partly hidden by the buildings of which the rear is shown. The sign 'Chest X-Ray' can be seen on the left of the latter's buildings. This was used for mass radiography to detect early signs of disease.

George L. Roberts

Park Row – Postern Street

This picture was taken in 1971 showing the junction of Park Row, on the left, with Postern Street at right angles to it. The bridge with the spire was a walkway across Postern Street – connecting two parts of the General Hospital. The building on the right is part of the hospital and is still there but all the other buildings have been demolished.

Ropewalk

This picture was taken in the 1930s and the main building was No. 34. It still remains and does not look much different today. The building on the left of No. 34 has had the small structures at the front removed and a new entrance made.

Nottingham City Council

THE 20TH-CENTURY EXTENSION OF THE CITY

The City Council started building council houses in 1920. Two large estates were built first, one at Sherwood and the other at Stockhill, Basford. Other smaller schemes followed but by 1925 the City Council built more large sites, as this meant the cost per house would be less. They did have one site to the west of Stockhill, which stretched as far as the city boundary. The City Council was able to buy the adjoining land and extended the Aspley Estate. They were able also to obtain further land outside the city at Bestwood and Colwick.

In 1932 it was generally agreed by both parties, the City and County councils, that it would be sensible if the lands outside the city where council houses were built could be made part of the city. An Act of Parliament was obtained in 1932 which sanctioned this.

The land to the west included the whole of Wollaton and Bilborough parishes and part of Strelley. Although not separate parishes, Broxtowe and Cinderhill were also part of the enlarged housing area. The Aspley Estate, Broxtowe, Bells Lane and part of Bilborough were built in the years up to 1939, when all forms of house building came to a halt. After the war Bilborough, Strelley and parts of Broxtowe became the sites of post-war schemes. This created a more or less new suburb in the north west.

Wollaton Hall and part of the land around it had been purchased by the City Council, which produced a small council estate on part of the land and some of the houses were offered for sale.

After the end of World War Two, the City Council took steps to find more land on which to build council houses as it had a long waiting list for them, particularly for those who had served in the armed forces. The City Council took the view that the north-west area was large enough and desired to expand southwards. The only large enough area likely to be available was Clifton. This was outside the city and moreover was south of the River Trent. The City Council were able to purchase the Clifton Estate yet it was several years before permission to build was obtained, but eventually a new council estate of about 7,000 houses became one of the largest estates in Britain.

Most of the land outside the city that was acquired was undeveloped and mainly agricultural land. Wollaton, Bilborough, Strelley, Clifton and Wilford, however, did have existing small villages. Some of these had existing houses, which would have been demolished anyway but the character of them was retained as far as possible. Wollaton, Clifton and Wilford have been conserved where possible with some appropriate developments. Bilborough village still has a small part of its original character and most of Strelley village remains in the county.

Thanks to a largely unknown band of photographers and artists, the Local Studies Library of Nottingham contains a number of images of which a selection has been used in this final chapter.

Aspley Hall

Aspley was part of the parish of Radford until the latter became part of the Borough of Nottingham in 1877. The hall was built about 1600 and was part of the Middleton estate until sold in 1925. It was demolished in 1968 and the site built on with new houses.

Nottingham City Council

Broxtowe Hall

'Broxtowe' is probably descended from 'Brocolvestu', the name of a weapontake mentioned in the *Domesday Book*. It was a meeting place of men of the district and not a village. The hall shown in the photograph dated 1925 was demolished in 1937 as part of the site of the Broxtowe council housing estate. Its position was on the edge of Broxtowe Wood, near Deepdene Way. The hall was built about 1700 and at one time was the home of Thomas Helwys, a leader of early Baptists.

Nottingham City Council

Aspley Lane

Aspley parish was partly in the city of Nottingham and partly in the county. In the late 1920s the City Council started to build council houses at Aspley, some of them on the land which it had purchased from the city under an Extension Act of 1932, and Aspley and other adjacent areas became wholly within the city. Aspley Estate was more or less completely built up by 1932 when this photograph was taken. It shows the junction of Aspley Lane with Melbourne Road (on the right), a wide road down to Nuthall Road.

Nottingham City Council

Christ Church, Nuthall Road

This church was built in 1855 on a site given by the Duke of Newcastle and the building was designed by T.C. Hine, one of Nottingham's most distinguished architects of the 19th century. The district was growing at the time with houses for the nearby Cinderhill Colliery workers.

Nottingham City Council

Cinderhill Lane/Nuthall Road

The photograph dated 15 May 1925 was taken from a point in the foreground of a lane, which later became Bells Lane. The chimneys in the background were in Cinderhill Colliery's grounds. There is now a large traffic roundabout there and a hotel has been built just beyond the trees on the right.

Napoleon Square

The two groups of houses were part of 59 houses built by Thomas North for miners at Cinderhill Colliery. They were bought by Nottingham Council in the 1950s and were demolished to form the site of Keverne Close. The track between the two house groups was formerly the mineral railway line.

Cinderhill Road

This photograph was taken on 11 July 1933 on Cinderhill Road looking south to Nuthall Road. The bridge was one of two, which carried railway lines from Basford to Kimberley.

Bells Lane

The estate was of council houses on Bells Lane, which runs from the traffic roundabout on Nuthall Road to Broxtowe Lane. The semi-detached houses with different roof styles were planned to give some variety to the street scene.

Player School

The Education Committee built two new large school complexes to serve the extensive north west of council houses on the Aspley, Bilborough, Broxtowe and Bells Lane estates. The one in the photograph shows one aspect of the Player School, the school clinic. This was part of the pioneering school medical service started in the 1920s.

Nottingham City Council

William Crane School

This new school, built on Minver Crescent, Aspley, was one of the new type of schools built by the City Council in the 1920s and 1940s. This one was William Crane School, named after a City Council Alderman who played a leading part in the council's Housing and Education Committees. He was knighted in 1959.

J. Orton

Adams Hill

This photograph was taken in the 1960s and shows a traffic census point. The enumerators seem to be using manual recording rather than the mechanical devices used later. The point was an opening from Adam's Hill to Derby Road.

Derby Road

This photograph has been dated as of the 1920s but the cars look more of the 1930s vintage. The Beeston Lodge on the right-hand side is opposite the start of Beeston Lane, a bus route through the university grounds to Beeston. In the 1960s this road was closed as a highway and became part of the university campus. Derby Road today is part of the A52 road.

The Square, Wollaton

The photograph shows the heart of the village with St Leonard's Church in the background. The row of old cottages on the right is very much the same as in 1907, when the photograph was taken. The Admiral Rodney public house on the left has been considerably altered since then.

Nottingham City Council

Lenton Lodge

The lodge was built at the Derby Road end of a drive to Wollaton Hall. It was designed by an eminent architect Sir Jeffry Wyatville. It was built in 1825 and it has been a residence and offices. The bridge in the bottom right-hand corner of the picture, taken in 1905, was over the River Leen

Nottingham City Council

Balloon Houses

These houses demolished in 1924 were situated on the edge of the parish at the junction of Trowell Road and Coventry Lane. The name of the houses and of a nearby wood were believed to have been given after an early 19th-century balloon ascent there. Modern houses are built on the site, after an ill-fated deck access estate, built in the 1960s, was demolished.

L. Cripwell

Vine Cottage, Wollaton Road

The photograph was thought to have been taken about 1905. There is now no trace of it, nor of the trees. That is not surprising, as after Wollaton became part of the city new houses were built along the whole of the west side of Wollaton Road from Russell Drive to the village.

Wollaton Road

This photograph was taken in the 1920s by F.W. Stevenson, who took many photographs of old Nottingham that were not only of high quality but also artistically conveyed the essence of his subjects. The house is still in existence and is a listed building.

F. Walden Stevenson

Clifton Village

Owned by the Clifton family for centuries, the village survived largely unchanged in 1907 when this photograph was taken. The village continued to remain that way despite being purchased as part of an estate on which to build some 7,000 council houses. It became part of the city in 1952 and today it is a conservation area.

Clifton Hall

A Grade I listed building, the hall is largely Georgian in character, but built on the site of a former house. After the City Council purchased the whole estate it was used for a time as a girls' grammar school then as a teacher's training college, part of Trent Polytechnic and later of Nottingham Trent University. It has since been sold and some new houses built in parts of the grounds.

Wells Almshouses

This group of almshouses, built in 1709, stands near the village green. The small building on the left is a gazebo and is matched by a similar one at the other end. The photograph was taken in 1951 when the City Council had purchased the estate. They have remained unchanged, protection being given as listed buildings. The founder was a George Wells.

Glapton

The official title of Clifton parish was Clifton-cum-Glapton. ('Cum' was Latin for 'with' – why did they use Latin?) This picture was taken in March 1958 when much of the new Clifton estate had houses built on it – some of them can be glimpsed in the picture. The old cottages were about to be demolished to make way for further council houses. The cottage with the chimney was a cruck cottage. An oak tree would be split down the middle and a spar joined them to form an 'A' shape on which a timber frame could be built.

Clifton from Glapton Lane
This was one of the many excellent photographs taken by F.W. Stevenson in 1933. Glapton Lane was on the east side of the road which divided it from Clifton.

The centre of the village
Clifton had a number of thatched cottages in the 1930s when this photograph was taken. A village 'industry' popular with visitors from Nottingham was the cottages, which supplied cream teas. The larger building was the estate manager's house, the third most important man after the squire and the rector.

Wilford

Wilford remained a rural village after 1877 when the part north of the River Trent became part of the borough. It was only a short distance from the borough and was a favoured resort for artists and photographers. This scene is probably where the village hall near the church is today.

Henry Kirk White's Cottage

This charming scene on the bank of the River Trent was drawn by Thomas Hammond in 1915. Henry Kirk White was born in 1785 and after working on a stocking frame became articled to a solicitor. He suffered ill-health but was able to attend Cambridge for a short time. He died of tuberculosis in 1815. He lived for a short time in the house bearing his name at Wilford and wrote poems which the poet Robert Southey had published. He also wrote the hymn *Oft in danger, oft in woe*'.

John Deane's Cottage

John Deane was born in Nottingham in 1679. He had a remarkably varied career as a captain in the Royal Navy, was the owner of a boat called the *Nottingham Galley*, which was shipwrecked, and later served in the Tsar of Russia's navy. A less adventurous later career saw him as a British Consul. After he retired he lived at Wilford where he died aged 82. There is a tomb in which he was buried in Wilford Churchyard.

Ruddington Lane

This photograph of thatched cottages was taken in 1905. Many of the cottages were the subject of picture postcards, picturesque but insanitary.

Main Road

This photograph of some of the better built houses was taken in 1900. The houses were opposite Bell Lane just a short distance from the crossroads.

Ferry Inn

This ancient inn is just south of the toll bridge and was named after the chain ferry, which operated before the bridge was built.